Advance Praise for Millennials' Guide to Marketing

"*Millennials' Guide to Marketing* offers practical insights into effective techniques for modern marketing campaigns. The explanations are easy to follow and accompanied by relevant examples and external materials so readers can actually use the tools described in the book."

-Shane Tinnin, COO and Founder of Skillway Sales Coaching

"As an entrepreneur with multiple businesses, I often have creative ideas for growth strategies. This guide offers practical how-to advice on actually implementing those ideas to receive meaningful results that drive revenue. Any small business owner would benefit from this tool."

**-Evane Stoner, Owner, Poppy & Peep Chocolate
Owner, Evane Stoner Interiors**

"Whether you are a small business owner or a veteran marketer, this book is truly your go-to guide for all things marketing. While our industry is ever-changing, this guide offers practical insights into the one thing that always remains the same: the foundational principles of communications and marketing."

-Macey Cleary Binner, Vice President, REED

MILLENNIALS' GUIDE TO MARKETING

What No One Ever Told You About
This Ever-Evolving Industry

WINDING PATHWAY BOOKS

Lauren Reed

Jennifer Poythress

Published by Winding Pathway Books

WINDING PATHWAY BOOKS

ISBN (print): 978-1-954374-11-9
ISBN (e-book): 978-1-954374-12-6

Book design by: Wendy C. Garfinkle
Cover artwork by Kayla Wood
Cover design by Wendy C. Garfinkle
Lauren's Photo Credit: Tausha Dickinson
Jennifer's Photo Credit: Tausha Dickinson

For more information or bulk orders, visit: www.millennialsguides.com

Printed in the United States of America

Contents

Foreword

I first met Lauren Reed in 2009, when my company, Paramore Digital, and the company she worked for at the time were pitching the same client for different pieces of business. We both won our respective contracts, mine for digital marketing and hers for public relations, and we sat sort of on the same side of the table with that client for three years. I didn't particularly care for Lauren at the time. She was, shall we say, high energy. At that time there was a larger divide between digital and public relations than there is now, but the gap was definitely closing. Everybody fought for their share of the pie, which is always only so large. This sets up some strange dynamics.

At some point during those three years I went to dinner with the owners of the company for which Lauren worked and they just would not shut up about how great she was. Finally I said, "You're going to have to enlighten me, because I don't get it."

They both laughed and said "Everybody who sits across the table from Lauren feels that way, but she's the best employee we've ever had. The brightest, the most productive, the hardest worker."

So I took a breath and began to look at Lauren in a different way; not as someone who was competing with her for more of our shared client's limited marketing budget, but as one professional to another.

Of course they were right.

When it was time for Lauren to leave that company, Paramore Digital became her first client and REED Public Relations was born. After I sold Paramore Digital and started coaching CEOs in the marketing industry, she became my first client, and on it goes. There are few people in the professional world that I know better than I know Lauren, and that's saying something because I know a lot of people, and there's a lot to know about her. Lauren has steadily built one of the most impressive public relations agencies in our market and beyond on the same tenacity, grit and determination I saw when I sat across the table from her in 2009. Few people in business can keep up with her. Nobody I've met can outrun her. Not very many of them even try.

In fact, this trait of moving fast and tirelessly might be why Lauren has been so successful with REED Public Relations. As with many industries, marcomm has been deeply impacted by the pace of change that digital brought about. Lauren's energy and drive mirror the industry and the tools she works with.

When Lauren told me she had been asked to write The Millennial's Guide to Marketing I thought, of course she had, and I knew that, just like with all the things she has on her crowded plate, this would be a winner too. I also knew she would have a great team behind the writing of this book and that is true as well. Jennifer Poythress was integral to the success of REED in the early days and was my account manager when we first became REED's client. Much of the content that has become this book came from Jennifer's work at the agency so it's tried and true. The stuff works.

Lauren straddles the GenX and Millennial generations, and because she has been self-supporting since she was a teenager, she also has some Boomer tendencies. This unique, albeit a little weird, blend of generational traits is spot on for her role in the professional world. It gives her a unique lens on the world of public relations and marketing as it has crossed over into the digital marketing space. Lauren is old-soul enough not to rely on technology to do the job that strategy should do, and Millennial enough to expect the very most from the constantly changing stream of tools at our disposal now. That combination is good because it's easy to mistake a good tactic, made possible by groovy tools, for a solid strategy.

If you're a Millennial and you've picked up this book, the last thing you need is guidance on digital tools. Your expectations are different from mine simply because of when you were born. Instead, you need to dive into the *why* behind every *how*. This book will help you with that. It's a textbook in bullet point format, long on strategy, short on digital directions. By the time you read this you'll be in the middle third of your career. It's time you learned this...

Strategy leads. Technology supports.

You'll learn that and much more as you dive into *The Millennial's Guide to Marketing*. Use it as a reference book. Write in it. Highlight it. Reread it. Require everyone on your team to have a copy. Absorb it, then put it to use in your business. You'll be glad you did.

Hannah Paramore Breen
Founder, Paramore Digital
Author of *Business Ownership: The Joy, The Pain, The Truth*

HOW TO USE THIS BOOK

If you've read *Millennials' Guide to Work*, *Millennials' Guide to Management and Leadership*, *Millennials' Guide to Relationships*, or any of the Millennials' Guides books, you know how this works. *Millennials' Guides* are not books best read cover to cover. We encourage you to review the table of contents and identify a challenge you are currently having or recently experienced. Turn to those pages to start finding answers!

Each challenge includes a brief description and several strategies you may want to try. Many times, you can see success after trying one option. You'll see some solutions repeated across different challenges because they're likely to be helpful for many problems. For complex challenges, you may want to attempt several interventions at the same time.

It's important to have patience and give the solutions a little bit of time to work. Some ideas that you try won't solve the problem but will make it a little better – that's still success! If you don't feel comfortable trying a solution or if it works partially or not at all, try something else. Some of the solutions are very low risk, such as drafting an informative column on your area of expertise for the local business journal. Others can appear more challenging, such as creating a digital marketing strategy for a new product launch or preparing a crisis communications plan for your organization. Start with solutions that feel like lower risk to you and work your way up to more challenging solutions.

Part I. Hint: PR Doesn't Stand for Press Release

Challenge 1: Defining the Industry

The marketing industry is in a constant state of evolution as the borders between each discipline are increasingly merging. The public relations function continuously converges with marketing. The divide between digital and traditional marketing is also breaking down, and separate disciplines are now being viewed as one. Paid and earned media strategies are developed around the same table versus the silos of years past. An integrated strategy is not only desirable, but it's necessary if you are to succeed in this industry. To fully understand, let's start by defining the difference between public relations and marketing.

1. **What is the goal of PR?** The goal of public relations is to create awareness and trust. The job of a PR professional is to communicate with audiences, directly or through intermediaries such as the media, to generate awareness of the company. Our desired outcome is a trusted relationship with our audience.

2. **What is the goal of marketing?** Marketing strives to create demand for products and services. The job of a marketer is to stimulate demand in an audience by triggering a response and a need and then position our products and services as solution to that need. Our desired outcome is an interested buyer.

3. **These are no longer separate disciplines, as public relations facilitates marketing.** It's anticipated that public relations will further evolve over the next five years by becoming even more closely aligned with marketing.

4. **So wait, PR doesn't stand for press release?** No, and in actuality, public relations is much more all-encompassing than you might realize. Check out this commonly used definition of PR from Cutlip, Center and Broom's *Effective Public Relations.*[1] ***"Public Relations is the management function that establishes and maintains mutually beneficial relationships between an organization and the publics on whom its success or failure depends."*** This definition was first published in 1952 and is still in print today in its eleventh edition, which clearly shows how despite our ever-evolving industry, the foundations of public relation remain unchanged.

5. **PR professionals often find themselves utilizing a wide variety of tactics to maintain these relationships and achieve their goals.** This might involve engaging in email marketing, coordinating event activations, working with influencers, pitching to media and much more (And yes, sometimes we write press releases).

6. **Embrace the PESO Model.** Created by Gini Dietrich in 2013, the PESO Model is a modern approach that converges *Paid*, *Earned*, *Shared* and *Owned* media. It essentially represents the merging of multiple disciplines into one unit for a well-rounded, integrated approach.

7. **The PR and marketing industries use very similar methods and some of the same tools.** A PR professional uses the media to create awareness, social media to communicate with audiences, publications to provide information to audiences and even advertising to drive awareness to content. PR professionals also rely on trusted third parties like news outlets and publications to create social proof and trust in an organization and its products and services.

8. **Marketers use similar tools to generate demand.** Marketers utilize social media to trigger need, pose questions and highlight the implicit problems audiences have that their company will solve. Marketers also use advertising to reach audiences that we can't reach organically. The driving purpose of their work is not awareness as much as it is demand generation.

9. **Awareness without demand is like having a restaurant that customers never visit.** Demand without awareness and trust is like having a great locale that customers can't find. PR and marketing should work together to generate demand and connect your audience with the source to satisfy their needs. Combined, they encourage people to tell each other about the restaurant, trust that the food is good, actually visit the location and order food.

10. **Whatever the tactic, you must be able to define results.** Marketers place a huge emphasis on accountability and return-on-investment (ROI). While public relations efforts traditionally strive to achieve brand awareness, tracking efforts and ability to directly correlate results has been a perceived weakness of the industry. This is an area where the PR industry can learn from their marketing counterparts.

11. **Marketing is more traditionally linked to sales and has consistently emphasized data and measurement.** Public relations can demonstrate its value most effectively by showing how its programs achieve measurable business outcomes and by improving its result measurement methods.

12. **Fundamental to measurement is having clear goals in place at the start.** Factors such as the rise of digital are allowing

us to connect results back to goals in a way that has never been done. As professionals in the PR and marketing space, we should take advantage of these tools to prove our value and achieve greater organizational success.

TAKE ACTION: Select a product, organization or issue. List out 2-3 ideas that could be either PR or marketing actions. Once the tactics are formulated, come up with 2-3 ways to measure success within this integrated campaign.

See also:
Challenge 11: Understanding Today's Media Landscape
Challenge 22: Defining Digital Marketing
Challenge 32: Defining Thought Leadership

Challenge 2: Working in the Industry

As the division between marketing and public relations continues to corrode due to the digital transformation and rise of social media, each area is becoming less of a specialty. The next generation of talent entering the job market will need to possess a broader skillset and recognize that marketing and public relations are increasingly co-mingling. This also means there will be more competition for jobs.

1. **When looking for a role in the PR and marketing spaces, possessing a strong business acumen is key.** Marketers place a huge emphasis on accountability and ROI. Public relations is no exception, and practitioners must be cognizant of the need for programs to be measurable. In both disciplines, it's crucial to stay mindful of how your tactics and strategies align with and benefit the organizations overarching business goals.

2. **It's also important to be nimble when looking for a job in this industry, as your ability to quickly adapt to new challenges will help you stand out from the competition.** Staying on top of the latest industry news and media trends will also prove to be beneficial. Essentially, you should always strive to evolve your skillset with the industry, as this will help you stand out amongst other potential candidates.

3. **Acquiring experience in both functions early in on your career, or while you are still in college, will also put you at a huge advantage.** If you have extra room in your schedule, consider taking both marketing and PR classes, as well as some business courses to bolster your business acumen. Writing for your school paper, interning with the university's PR department, finding internships and joining nationally recognized PR and marketing associations are also great ways to network and gain hands-on marketing and writing experience while you are still in school.

4. **Writing skills remain key.** This is critical for success in the marketing and PR industry. We write pitches, press releases, op-eds, bylined columns, social media content, website copy (and lots and lots of emails). If you are a strong writer and take steps to continue to grow in this space, you will go far in this industry.

5. **Another trait that will set you up for success is the ability to stay curious and be a lifelong learner.** In both PR and marketing, chances are you will end up working on a wide variety of projects across a myriad of different industries. Throughout this process, there will likely be some industries that you gravitate to more than others, but possessing the willingness to engage with and dive deep into each one that comes your way will allow you to grow and excel.

6. **The willingness to be a lifelong learner will also help boost your creativity.** It is often thought that our industry is full of the stereotypical "creative" types. However, what we have found is that a sharp business mind combined with a desire to learn is what leads to the most productive brainstorming and creative concepts.

TAKE ACTION: Write your dream job description. List out the skills required. Rank yourself in each area. Where do you stand? Seek out resources in areas you need to grow.

See Also:
Challenge 11: Understanding Today's Media Landscape
Challenge 15: Working With Media (Do's and Don'ts)
Challenge 19: Working With Content Creators & Influencers (Do's and Don'ts)
Challenge 54: Practicing Ethical Marketing

Part II: Preparation / Planning

Challenge 3: How Do I Begin?

The later sections of this book will address tactics – also known as the fun stuff. The most important stuff, however, is the foundational work. No matter how many new tools, widgets, and gadgets you have access to, you'll always want to refer back to the industry basics that have been around for more than 100 years.

1. **Different organizations and different authors use different acronyms:** RACE (Research and Planning, Action, Communication, Evaluation), ROPE (Research, Objectives, Programming, Evaluation), or RPIE (Research, Planning, Implementation, Evaluation). For the purposes of this book, we will use RPIE. You can find a more detailed breakdown of this process in the APR study guide on the Public Relations Society of America (PRSA) website[2].

2. **Whichever acronym you prefer, they all refer to a four-step process that will help you achieve your overarching goals:** (1) Research/analysis of the situation, (2) Planning, goal/objective setting, (3) Implementation/execution/communication, and (4) Evaluation.

3. **It is vital to start at the beginning.** Seems obvious, right? But it can be tempting to skip the planning stages in favor of the flashy execution stages. You cannot effectively solve a problem or initiate tactics without proper research. Take the time to fully understand what you are working with and what success looks like so that your fun, creative ideas can actually contribute to your organization's goals.

4. **Step One is research.** Research is arguably the most important part of the RPIE process, as this stage will guide all your strategies and tactics moving forward. Good research aims to answer the following: WHO do we want to reach? WHAT

do we want people in each target market to DO? WHAT messages do we want to communicate to each of these audiences that will increase knowledge, change opinions and encourage desired behavior?

5. **Step Two is planning.** Guided by your research findings, it's time to put pen to paper and determine how you will reach your target audience to have the desired effect. Five elements should form the framework of your plan:
   - **Goals.** What are the long-term goals of your organization and how will this campaign help to achieve them? Limit the number of goals you set. Identify no more than three to five. One may be enough.
   - **Publics/Audiences:** Identify the groups you want to communicate with. These target audience(s) should be clearly defined and grouped together by what they have in common.
   - **Objectives:** Phrase objectives in terms of specific results you desire and what you think is possible. Each objective should cite an audience, outcome, attainment level (%) and time frame. (Example: To have 65 percent of new visitors to your website complete a purchase at the end of six months.)
   - **Strategies:** How will you reach your objectives? You will probably have several strategies per objective. Examples of strategies could be to engage community influencers or to drive traffic to your website.
   - **Tactics:** These are the specific tools you'll use to execute your strategies. Tactics can include securing paid or earned media spots, exhibiting at trade shows or community events, Pay Per Click (PPC) ad buys, meeting with key officials or developing other strategic partnerships, to name a few. You can have several tactics per strategy.

6. **Step Three is implementation.** Time for action! Implementing a marketing plan effectively means executing all tactics on time, staying in budget and knowing who is responsible for each piece. Monitor progress as you go so you can course-correct and adapt rather than solely reviewing the results at the end.

7. **Step Four is Evaluation.** A campaign isn't complete with a postmortem. Whether you landed the results you were hoping for or not, evaluation is key to understanding which objectives were met, which were not and what can be improved or expanded upon next time. Often, the evaluation from one campaign becomes part of the initial research for a future campaign.

TAKE ACTION: List three goals for your next marketing campaign and how you will measure them. Be specific and realistic.

See also:
Challenge 6: Be S.M.A.R.T! Setting Measurable Goals and Objectives
Challenge 7: Research & Data Analytics
Challenge 12: Creating an Effective Media List
Challenge 16: Developing Content & Telling a Compelling Story

Challenge 4: Your Message Matters – How Do You Know You're on the Right Track?

How an organization acts and appears to the world during both critical situations and in everyday communication has the potential to impact your brand for years to come – for better or worse. You have an opportunity to make a good impression by creatively communicating with grace and professionalism. The following process takes you through every step of ensuring you are on the right track when developing your marketing message.

1. **Identify your stakeholders.** Who is impacted by your organization and why? Some examples might be your customers, employees, investors, or the local community you serve.

2. **Assess audience sentiment.** How do you want each audience to think of you six months after a big announcement or campaign? Defining how you want to be portrayed in the future should guide your immediate communications.

3. **Create a tactical plan.** How will you reach each audience? Think about how complex or simple your message is and choose tactics that accordingly. For example, a tech company may exhibit their product at a trade show while a chef or food company may see more success engaging food bloggers on social media. A good tactical plan determines how to disseminate your message and what content needs to be created to get it done.

4. **Cross-check your marketing message with your organization's overall mission.** Is everything in alignment with the organization's core values? If not, your marketing isn't contributing to your overarching business goals.

5. **Develop brand filters to ensure your marketing message doesn't drift.** With the leadership team, decide on 3-5 statements that will serve as a litmus test to run ALL communications through. This will keep your message on track regardless of the strategies and tactics being used to execute.

TAKE ACTION: To hold your own brand filters session most effectively, key members of the leadership and marketing teams should set aside 3 or 4 hours to develop the statements that will guide every marketing and communications message from your organization. Download a free brand filters worksheet at www.reedpublicrelations.com/millennialsguide.

See Also:
Challenge 10: Developing Key Messages
Challenge 18: Knowing What Platforms to Use
Challenge 55: Pursuing Measurable Results

Challenge 5: I Have My Message! What's Next?

Armed with a strong marketing message, you're almost ready to distribute to the masses. But knowing where to put your message is crucial, especially when time and budget are limited. Modern marketers are finally adopting the PESO model, which was created by Gini Dietrich in 2014. This approach converges Paid, Earned, Shared and Owned media to create an integrated marketing campaign[3].

1. **Paid media refers to any channels that require payment for placement.** This could be social media advertising, sponsored content or email marketing.

2. **Earned media is typically associated with public relations.** It's content that is strategically placed rather than paid for. Examples include press releases, bylined columns, unpaid product features, leadership profiles and more. Earned media can be especially effective because it increases brand awareness, credibility and search engine optimization all at the same time.

3. **Shared media focuses on social media.** This can include any number of social media platforms from Instagram to Reddit, but you don't need to be active on all of them. Find out where your target audiences are and focus on producing great content and being engaging there.

4. **Owned media is specifically content an organization produces and distributes on its own.** This could be websites and landing pages, a blog or a podcast.

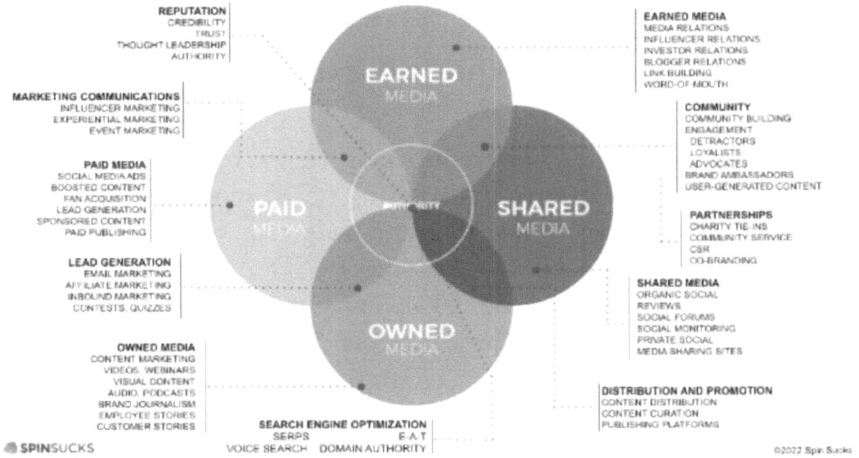

The PESO Model™, Spin Sucks, 2013

TAKE ACTION: Brainstorm ideas for each piece of the PESO model and create a Venn diagram like the one below.

See also:
Challenge 4: Your Message Matters – How Do You Know You're on the Right Track?
Challenge 12: Creating an Effective Media List
Challenge 16: Developing Content & Telling a Compelling Story

Challenge 6: Be S.M.A.R.T! Setting Measurable Goals and Objectives

Because marketing is a tool of business, you should be able to connect your marketing goals back to the overarching business goals of your organization. If you want to achieve those goals, you have to be smart – or S.M.A.R.T. – about it. S.M.A.R.T. goals and objectives look like this:

1. **Specific.** Be specific about what action will be taken and which of your target audiences it will involve. Being specific at the onset will keep the team focused even in the thick of execution when things can get hectic.

2. **Measurable.** Use tangible metrics that can be quantified. Determine key performance indicators (KPIs) that are trackable such as landing page conversion rates or levels of engagement on social media. Use percentages ("Increase follower engagement on TikTok by 30 percent within 3 months") to define goals clearly and concisely.

3. **Achievable.** Be ambitious but realistic. Determining what is achievable is most easily done by reviewing past initiatives. If you don't have data from previous campaigns for comparison, you will have to estimate until a baseline is set. Consider your available resources and how much time you have to achieve the set goals.

4. **Relevant.** All goals should tie back to your organization's overarching mission. Hitting a marketing goal isn't a win unless it contributes to the bigger picture.

5. **Time-specific.** Set a timeline and stick to it. Make sure you can achieve measurable results within the time you have and

designate long-term vs. short-term goals. Short-term goals can be achieved in 30-60 days. Long-term goals will take at least six months – but more likely a year – to accomplish.

6. **Remember that effectively communicating your results back to the leadership team is just as important as setting S.M.A.R.T goals.** Evaluating campaigns and conveying the results will help justify (or increase) your marketing budget and serve as the initial research for the next campaign.

TAKE ACTION: Review your current marketing goals and try to fit them into the S.M.A.R.T model. If you are missing a piece, what needs to be done to adjust that goal to be S.M.A.R.T?

See also:
Challenge 7: Research and Data Analytics
Challenge 18: Knowing What Platforms to Use
Challenge 55: Pursuing Measurable Results

Challenge 7: Research and Data Analytics

"Marketing research is the function that links the consumer, customer, and public to the marketer through information—information used to identify and define marketing opportunities and problems; generate, refine, and evaluate marketing actions; monitor marketing performance; and improve understanding of marketing as a process." –*American Marketing Association*[4]

1. **Successful marketing campaigns are based on research-driven strategies and tactics.** The beginning of a campaign is not when the first initiative is executed but when the research behind that initiative begins.

2. **Familiarize yourself with types of research and identify which methodology will be most beneficial for guide your marketing strategies.**
   - **Primary vs. Secondary:** Primary research requires you to conduct your own interviews, surveys or focus groups to create data on your target market or audience while secondary research refers to studies conducted by other reputable sources. Reliable data sources for secondary research can include government data from entities such as the U.S. Census Bureau, published annual reports from major companies, trade association reports and verifiable market research reports already conducted by other organizations.
   - **Formal vs. Informal:** Formal research uses a systematic approach that can be replicated with a larger group to produce the same results (i.e. the scientific method). This can be costly and you may not have the budget or time with every new marketing venture, but it will give you the most unbiased and scalable data. Informal research takes less time and money, but it could lead to more biases in your results. It refers to any nonscientific method of

gathering data such as conducting phone surveys or focus groups with a target demographic.

- **Quantitative vs. Qualitative:** In short, quantitative is about nailing down numbers and qualitative is about discovering motivation. The goal of quantitative research is to end up with statistical data representative of an entire population, but it can be difficult for businesses to get a large enough sample size for accurate quantitative data without the help of a secondary source (see above). Qualitative research, on the other hand, looks more at the psychology behind people's choices and the emotions that drive their decisions. This is often done in moderated focus groups or by collecting comments from the target consumer in other ways such as online community groups or existing product reviews.

3. **Consider the following questions as you determine which methodologies will be used for your research:**
    - What decision will be made from research results, and what information is required to support the decision?
    - What resources and budget are available for information gathering?
    - What other parts of your organization — or other organizations — have already done research you could use?
    - Does sample selection for a survey give you an accurate assessment of your target population?
    - How big is your sample and universe/survey population?
    - How will you collect data — surveys, interviews, focus groups? In-person or via telephone, mail or online?
    - How much time do you have?
    - How scientific do you need to be; what level of confidence do you need to have in the data?
    - What questions will you ask?

- Will the results be used internally only, or will results be made public? How will you tabulate answers?

4. **Information gathering usually begins with an analysis of relevant secondary sources.** Sometimes secondary research is all you have the time or money to do. The key considerations in determining the scope of research you need are (1) what you need to find out and (2) how you plan to use research results. While secondary research may be enough in some situations, you will usually need primary research to establish benchmarks for assessing specific outcomes.

5. **In Steps 1 and 2 of the RPIE process (see Part II, Challenge 3), you'll do "formative" research.** It provides background on the current situation, guides planning, and signals needs for adjustments in program implementation. In Step 4, you'll do "summative" research. It assesses outcomes at the end of a program and may become "formative" research that establishes benchmarks for the next program.

TAKE ACTION: Determine which type of research will give the best insights into your audience's buying decisions. Do you need to conduct primary qualitative research? Can you pull secondary quantitative data from an existing study to save time and money?

See Also:
Challenge 3: How Do I Begin?
Challenge 8: Determining Your Target Audiences
Challenge 55: Pursuing Measurable Results
Challenge 54: Implementing Tools to Measure Your Success

Challenge 8: Determining Target Audiences

A well-crafted marketing message pushed to the wrong audience is not so well-crafted at all. For better or for worse, online data collection has made it easier than ever for brands to pinpoint where their audiences are and deliver tailored messaging directly to them. Still, you need to understand who your target audience is to properly utilize this data to reach them.

1. **Think about your ideal customer.** Is your product or service specifically for men or women? Which age group benefits from it? If your target age group skews younger (or elderly), who is making the purchasing decisions for them? How do you get in front of both the user of your product or service and the person buying it for them?

2. **Price point plays a part.** How expensive is your product or service? Does your ideal customer need to fall into a certain income class to afford you? Maybe your goal is to attract a lower income bracket.

3. **Pull data on these demographics.** Use past digital campaigns to see which demographics are engaging with your content most and who is converted to a paying customer most often. You can use this data to retarget ads or tailor future content for them. If starting fresh, pull statistics on your ideal customer from government agencies or local community groups that typically have demo data available and free to view.

TAKE ACTION: List 3-5 characteristics your ideal customer has based on the criteria above.

See also:
Challenge 7: Research & Data Analytics
Challenge 21: Finding Micro-Influencers to Fit Your Niche
Challenge 36: Finding a Cause That Aligns With Your Brand
Challenge 51: Preparing for International Campaigns

Challenge 9: Communications Audit

A communications audit provides information on how to better communicate with your audiences. It's the process of reviewing all existing content to gauge how effectively each material speaks to the desired audience. This will help determine what new content needs to be created and what needs to be edited to stay timely. You are checking that messaging is accurate, culturally appropriate, and effective in meeting your marketing goals.

1. **Review the core pieces of your marketing & PR kit.** This may include the company boilerplate, backgrounder, fact sheets, leadership bios, current campaign messages, brochures, internal communications pieces, and other collateral materials.

2. **Do a digital audit.** Your online presence matters just as much, if not more, than your traditional media materials. Look for consistency across your website, social media channels, email communications, digital ads, and online influencer partnerships. Additionally, look at your digital location – where are you appearing online, and does it still make sense to be in that digital space?

3. **Audit effectiveness.** Sending email surveys to a target audience is a great way to get feedback about if the desired message is getting through. Tools like SurveyMonkey make it easy to send quick surveys that are low-effort and anonymous for responders, so they are more likely to be honest and direct. Depending on your audience, ask specific questions like, "How do you prefer to receive information from us?" or "Where have you seen (brand) in the last six months?" with answer choices being your current paid ad locations or something similar. Many survey services allow you to pull the data into a spreadsheet or chart for easy analysis.

4. **Audit every six months – if not more.** Things change and your communications materials should too. An audit should be done at least every six months under typical, business-as-usual conditions. During major societal shifts like a global pandemic, civil conflicts, or a big change within the company such as a merger or acquisition, you'll need to audit more frequently – maybe once a month – to avoid appearing tone deaf or sharing inaccurate information.

5. **Review your competitors.** Choose 3-5 true competitors (those targeting the same ideal customers and at similar price point) and analyze their current messaging, positioning and tactics. Where are they appearing online and are they seeing engagement from their followers? What traditional media are they appearing in and with what message? Take stock of the competition to get a better idea of where you stand in the marketplace.

TAKE ACTION: Create a series of spreadsheets to measure effectiveness, designating one spreadsheet for each of your marketing platforms. Include relevant questions analyzing your performance and give a "grade" of complete or incomplete for each question. Then add a column for proposed improvements and general comments.

See also:
Challenge 10: Developing Key Messages
Challenge 12: Creating an Effective Media List
Challenge 13: Writing Compelling Pitches & Press Releases
Challenge 24: Website Layout / Design

Challenge 10: Developing Key Messages

Key messages are how an organization positions itself and the value it brings to the rest of the world. They are the core takeaways you want a target audience to remember about your brand. Modern marketing campaigns may use a dozen tactics across multiple different platforms, but the key messages should remain consistent throughout.

1. **Key messages aren't just descriptions of what you do.** They should be more closely related to the business value proposition. Address your ideal customer's pain points and how the product or service provides a solution. What's in it for them?

2. **Keep it concise.** A key message statement should be one sentence that summarizes the value you bring to your customer. Avoid technical phrases and jargon. If you are writing key messages for the first time, don't get bogged down in getting the wording exactly right. Keep it simple and refine from there.

3. **Cross-check your marketing messages with your organization's mission.** Do your key messages support the organization's core values? If not, make some tweaks so they are in alignment.

4. **Develop brand filters to ensure your marketing message doesn't drift.** With the executive leadership team, decide on 3-5 statements that will serve as a litmus test to run ALL communications through. This will keep your message on track regardless of the strategies and tactics being used to execute.

5. **Get everyone on the same page.** Once key messages are developed, distribute them to the entire team to ensure everyone is on the same page.

TAKE ACTION: Brainstorm key message concepts with your leadership team with a word association game. Take turns listing words and phrases that you want to be associated with your brand and use the results to draft 3-5 key messages. Remember these are just rough drafts and more thought will be required to refine your final messaging.

See Also:
Challenge 4: Your Message Matters – How Do You Know You're on the Right Track?
Challenge 5: I Have My Message! What's Next?
Challenge 36: Finding a Cause That Aligns With Your Brand

Part III: Tactics

Section 1: Media Relations

Media relations is considered the bread and butter of public relations. It typically refers to securing unpaid news coverage – or earned media – in traditional outlets such as newspapers and TV. In an age where marketing and public relations are increasingly overlapping, a successful media relations campaign also helps bolster SEO, brand awareness and credibility online.

Challenge 11: Understanding Today's Media Landscape

If this were a Baby Boomer's Guide to Marketing, we might have to talk about how dedicated news times are gone (and not coming back) in favor of the 24-hour news cycle. Most Millennials have a good understanding of this shift, but not always a good grasp on the *speed* at which the modern 24-hour news cycle is running.

1. **Media outlets are being pushed to produce more content across more platforms faster than ever.** This comes with some challenges. Ensuring accuracy can be difficult when journalists are moving so quickly. Wrong information spreads fast, and you need to be diligent in catching coverage as soon as it is published to check for errors.

2. **The shelf-life of a story can be fleeting.** A constant overturn of stories "above-the-scroll" means your earned media coverage can get buried before it's had a chance to make an impression. Find ways to get more longevity out of coverage by utilizing social media, blogs and print media that tends to stick around longer than online content.

3. **It's not all bad for brands.** When media publish stories online, it leads to higher search engine rankings, more website clicks and ultimately higher conversion rates.

4. **A press release is still the go-to for major announcements to media and the public.** Whether distributed through one-to-one emails with journalists or pushed out over a paid wire service, the press release is still the primary tool used to share official news with media.

5. **If traditional media doesn't run a story, go elsewhere.** When natural disasters or public safety threats occur, they can dominate the news cycle and push your story to the backburner. Traditional media isn't the only way to reach our audiences anymore. A tweet can be seen as just a reputable as a story in a major news outlet and you can speak directly to your audience. Lean on social media channels, e-newsletters and paid marketing opportunities when earned media isn't an option.

TAKE ACTION: Start each day by monitoring news sites and their social accounts. This practice will keep you in tune with the news cycle, what's being covered and how quickly.

See Also:
Challenge 1: Defining the Industry
Challenge 33: Why Thought Leadership? (You're Already an Expert, Why Not Share What You Know?)
Challenge 34: Securing Op-Eds and Speaking Opportunities

Challenge 12: Creating an Effective Media List

At the core of media relations is 'relations,' of course. Unlike paid advertising or sales, media relations depend heavily on developing quality relationships with writers, editors and producers. A curated media list is one of a savvy PR professional's most valued assets. A media list is a comprehensive overview of who will be contacted at which media outlets during a campaign.

1. **Create a spreadsheet with target publications, target writers or editors and contact information.** A contact email and phone number is enough to suffice for basic news distribution, but if your campaign involves delivering samples or press kits to journalists, be sure to include a mailing or delivery address too.

2. **Utilize media databases such as Cision, MuckRack, and Factiva.** While these services come with a cost, they can be extremely helpful in identifying specific topics and locations that media outlets cover. You can pull reporter contact info, the beat they typically cover and readership or viewership numbers. However, the databases can sometimes be out-of-date so always double-check the outlet's website to ensure a writer hasn't changed beats or left their position.

3. **Note short-lead vs. long-lead.** Within your media list, separate short-lead outlets such as daily newspapers and local TV news from long-lead opportunities like print magazines and book features. Print magazines typically work on their issues 4 to 6 months in advance, so if you want to be included in the print edition of Southern Living's Holiday Gift Guide, for example, you'll need to be pitching in July.

4. **Update your media list as you reach out.** A media list is not a stagnant document but a living ledger of how media pitching is going during a campaign. On your spreadsheet, include a column for updates on when initial pitches went out, responses and next steps if an interview or coverage is secured.

TAKE ACTION: Create a master media list with separate tabs for different media types (local newspapers, regional news sites, national magazines, radio, etc.). Designate one column for each contact's beat so you can easily build future media lists for specific campaigns by pulling from the master list.

See also:
Challenge 8: Determining Target Audiences
Challenge 15: Working With Media
Challenge 34: Securing Op-Eds and Speaking Opportunities

Challenge 13: Writing Compelling Pitches & Press Releases

Journalists receive dozens, if not hundreds, of pitches and press releases every day. It can be easy to get lost in the shuffle, but there are a few ways to get noticed (and get published).

1. **Get to the point.** Writers work on deadlines and typically won't spend the time combing through a pitch or press release that doesn't get to the good stuff quickly. Avoid lengthy paragraphs that create blocks of text and instead opt for succinct snippets that convey the important information and will keep their attention. In pitch emails, use bullet points to share key points then include a full press release or link to a website landing page elsewhere.

2. **Pitch the right person and give them something valuable.** As with anything in marketing, research plays a key role here. Take the time to build a media list that includes relevant media outlets, writers and their beats. Understanding the type of news they cover and giving them something of real value to report is essential to earning coverage.

3. **Put your ask in your pitch.** What do you want them to do with the information you just shared? Are you offering to arrange an interview with a company spokesperson? Do you simply want them to share the news on their website? Wrap up pitch emails with a question such as, "Would you be interested in talking with our CEO, (name here), more about this news?"

4. **Be responsive and accessible when you get a bite.** If a journalist wants to move forward with an interview or sends a list of follow-up questions, be timely with a response. Be

sure to have a designated spokesperson who is media-trained and well-versed on the topic they will be speaking on before you start pitching. Always ask for a writer or producer's deadline if they don't share it to ensure you don't miss the opportunity.

TAKE ACTION: Write a pitch template that can be customized and sent to multiple outlets as needed. This should include a greeting, one sentence about the brand, a short paragraph giving the description of the story (use bullet points if it's too wordy), your ask and a sign-off.

See also:
Challenge 9: Communications Audit
Challenge 16: Developing Contant & Telling a Compelling Story
Challenge 34: Securing Op-Eds and Speaking Opportunities
Challenge 50: Taking Control of the Story

Challenge 14: Securing Interviews & Interview Prep

With newsroom employment numbers dropping steadily since 2008 according to Pew Research Center[5], landing a media interview is more of an art than a science. Acing that interview can be even more of a challenge.

1. **Be a resource.** Even if you aren't actively pitching a story, be ready to be a resource for media as timely events occur. For example, if you represent a bank and a major financial crisis is unfolding, you could offer up a top executive to comment as a local expert. Being a resource for journalists rather than constantly giving them a sales pitch builds trust and adds value to their stories.

2. **Connect journalists with authoritative sources that can offer with real insights.** Your organization's media contacts should be in relevant positions for the story you are pitching.

3. **Meet journalists where they are – unless they want to meet where you are.** Depending on the outlet, some reporters are expected to produce 2 to 3 news stories every day. Be flexible and open to phone or video interviews, responding to questions via email or meeting at a mutual destination. You should always have a few pre-approved locations in mind in case they want to come to you for a TV interview or facility tour.

4. **Create an interview prep document for the spokesperson.** This should include details about the journalist and media outlet they will be speaking with, topics that will be covered, potential questions to anticipate and logistical information about where and when the interview will be held. The

spokesperson should be as prepared as possible and equipped with the most up-to-date information going into the interview.

5. **Media training is important.** Proper media training teaches a spokesperson how to talk clearly and confidently during an interview, how to handle touchy issues with poise and even what to wear (i.e. avoid wearing stripes on TV). A helpful practice can be filming mock interviews and reviewing the footage to see how someone is coming across on camera and what can be improved upon.

6. **Have a press kit ready.** Don't wait until a reporter needs a hi-res version of the company logo or CEO headshot to track it down. Create a digital press kit with logos, relevant photos, a copy of the press release, fact sheets and other assets from your organization. Be sure the assets are well-labeled and easy to access.

TAKE ACTION: Make a list of who within your organization is media-trained and in an executive position to be a quality source for a reporter.

See Also:
Challenge 5: I Have My Message! What's Next?
Challenge 12: Creating an Effective Media List
Challenge 13: Writing Compelling Pitches & Press Releases
Challenge 34: Securing Op-Eds and Speaking Opportunities

Challenge 15: Working With Media (Do's and Don'ts)

Understanding how modern reporters and editors operate is crucial to getting their attention and placing stories.

1. **Do provide value.** When pitching news reporters, give them something worth reporting. If you are pitching more of a fluff piece, figure out how to make it relevant for the writer you are reaching out to or re-examine your media strategy to focus on profile pieces or product features rather than hard news coverage.

2. **Do give them a call if they don't respond.** Ah, the dreaded phone call. Most millennials hate phone calls, but if a journalist hasn't responded to your emails, it's time to pick up the phone. They receive hundreds of emails a day, and it's possible your story is a great fit but got buried in their inbox.

3. **Do meet journalists where they are – unless they want to meet where you are.** Depending on the outlet, some reporters are expected to produce 2 to 3 news stories every day. Be flexible and open to phone or video interviews, responding to questions via email or meeting at a mutual destination. But you should also have a few pre-approved locations in mind in case they want to come to you for a TV interview or facility tour.

4. **Don't pitch a story that is not relevant to their beat or publication.** Journalists are on deadline and have inboxes bursting with story pitches. Don't bury the lead – get right to the point in your pitch and make sure it is relevant to the news they usually cover.

5. **Don't keep pushing if you've already been told no.** This can be a hard one for traditional marketers or advertisers. News outlets have no obligation to use any story you pitch and harassing a reporter when they have already passed can damage the relationship and affect how they receive future stories from you. Sometimes it's best to re-route and try to get coverage elsewhere.

TAKE ACTION: Follow your media targets – both outlets and individual journalists – on their social channels and see what they are sharing. Get familiar with the areas they cover and the types of pieces they typically write.

See Also:
Challenge 13: Writing Compelling Pitches & Press Releases
Challenge 14: Securing Interviews & Interview Prep
Challenge 34: Securing Op-Eds and Speaking Opportunities
Challenge 50: Taking Control of the Story

Section 2: Social Media

Social media gives us the 'Shared Media' piece of the PESO Model. With a seemingly endless number of ways to share, knowing which platforms to be on, what content to create there and how to measure success can be a challenge.

Challenge 16: Developing Content & Telling a Compelling Story

Creating social media content takes more than writing a quippy tweet or two each week. Well-rounded social media accounts should be a means of digital storytelling for an organization. This can be through behind-the-scenes sneak peeks, team spotlights or any other number of ways to show the human side of a brand.

1. **Engagement is the name of the game.** As much as social media is a numbers game, it's also about quality. Having loyal, engaged followers is more important than the quantity of followers. Make content shareable, invite followers to be a part of a conversation or create downloadable resources that are useful to them, not just promotional for you. All these things encourage real engagement rather than just an increased follower count.

2. **Develop content based on how it will be distributed.** Content that works well on Facebook may not get the same response on Twitter. Content pieces should be customized to inspire optimal engagement on each platform.

3. **Create a monthly content calendar.** A simple spreadsheet with publish dates and times, copy and images or videos for each post will ensure posts are being made consistently and help you stay on track with your overall social media strategy. Once content is planned, there are several software options such as Hootsuite for scheduling posts in advance. Be sure to keep an eye on scheduled posts in case they need to be adjusted to account for timely events or cultural shifts.

4. **Pull from content pieces you already have.** If you have a company blog, media coverage or another marketing collateral piece like a well-designed fact sheet or graphic, get more traction out of it by sharing to social.

5. **Be consistent.** The story you tell on social should be consistent with the messaging on your website and in all other marketing pieces. Visually, social media content should have a nice, cohesive feel that aligns with the organization's overall branding.

TAKE ACTION: Create a posting schedule for your social media platforms. This could be every Monday, Wednesday, and Friday across all platforms or once a week on a particular account. Look at each page's analytics to determine the best days and times to post.

See Also:
Challenge 9: Communications Audit
Challenge 10: Developing Key Messages
Challenge 13: Writing Compelling Pitches & Press Releases

Challenge 17: Growing Your Reach and Following

In the good ol' days, one $20 Facebook ad would lead to 100 new page likes and a dozen click-throughs to a brand's website. Unfortunately, purely organic growth has become more difficult as most social media platforms have restructured to rely on paid ads as a primary revenue source. But there are still some scrappy ways to build a following with a limited budget.

1. **Find the right mix of paid and organic growth.** In today's social media landscape, you will likely need to utilize some paid advertising to get noticed. Modern algorithms prioritize paid content over everything else and can even hide your unpaid posts from your existing followers. Encourage organic growth by posting regularly and interacting with followers or other like-minded pages while also using paid advertising to target users who already have an interest in your niche.

2. **Post useful/educational content in addition to promotional content.** Build trust by showing you are a resource and an expert in your field by sharing tips, tricks, and tools that followers can actually use on your pages. The golden rule is 80/20: 80 percent of your posts should be generally helpful content and 20 percent can be promotional or sales driven.

3. **Post content based on how it will be distributed.** Content that works well on Facebook may not get the same response on Twitter. Content pieces should be customized to inspire optimal engagement on each platform.

4. **Beware paying for followers.** Some software companies claim to grow your following by X percent, but they are really just leading bots to follow your account. A high follower count is great, but real, engaged followers are better. That's what will drive actual sale conversions from your pages.

TAKE ACTION: Pull together 3 to 5 evergreen content pieces that are genuinely helpful for your followers. Provide them with something of value for free to build trust and position your brand as a resource for them.

See Also:
Challenge 8: Determining Target Audiences
Challenge 22: Defining Digital Marketing
Challenge 41: Finding Your Audience and Growing Your Listenership

Challenge 18: Knowing What Platforms to Use

The rule of thumb on social media is the same as most other areas of marketing and PR: go where your audience is – and nowhere else! Resist the urge to be on all platforms all the time. Spreading your message across too many platforms means it won't be optimized for any of them. Instead, aim to create stellar content on 2 to 3 platforms that is curated for your audience and tailored to how each platform functions.

1. **Follow the statistics to find your audience.** Age is one of the key indicators of where you should be on social. Facebook is the preferred platform for Baby Boomers (and some Millennials) while Gen Z and younger stick to Instagram, Snapchat and TikTok. Millennials can also be found on Twitter, but almost all generations meet in the middle on YouTube with it being the most used online platform in 2021, according to Pew Research Center's 2021 social media use survey[6].

2. **Regardless of where you are, video is king.** Even on platforms attracting older crowds like Facebook, video content is one of the most effective marketing tools on social. In fact, 88 percent of consumers said watching a brand's video convinced them to make a purchase or subscribe to a service, according to a 2021 Wyzowl study[7]. Many people are perusing social on mobile and often without sound, though, so don't forget to add captions or at least enable auto-generated captions to your videos.

3. **Keep tabs on the Meta conglomerate: Facebook, Instagram, WhatsApp, Oculus VR and more.** Whether you are a Facebook fan or not, there's no denying their role in modern marketing. The parent company, Meta Platforms, now owns

some of the largest media companies in the world as they attempt to create a metaverse that merges reality with virtual and augmented reality. How marketing and advertising will be fully utilized in the metaverse remains to be seen.

4. **LinkedIn has a place.** For B2B marketing, there's almost no better place than LinkedIn. LinkedIn should be used to promote thought leadership columns, company updates and team spotlights as well as to engage with others' content in a genuinely helpful way. Interact with colleagues in your industry, share interesting articles and offer non-salesy advice to demonstrate your expertise.

TAKE ACTION: Conduct a social media audit. Review what platforms you are currently using and think about your goals for each account. Evaluate whether your existing strategy is working. Then think about what approved assets you already have such as images, graphics, blogs, etc. and what needs to be created to ensure you have quality content to share.

See Also:
Challenge 8: Determining Target Audiences
Challenge 19: Working With Content Creators & Influencers
Challenge 41: Finding Your Audience and Growing Your Listenership
Challenge 46: Finding What Works Best for Your Team

Section 3: Influencer Relations

They say a picture is worth a thousand words, but is it worth $1,000? That depends on who the post is coming from. As the media landscape continues to change, the people telling your story are changing as well. Influencer campaigns have proven to be extremely effective even when traditional media has struggled to gain its footing in the digital world.

Challenge 19: Working with Content Creators & Influencers (Do's and Don'ts)

While working with influencers can produce similar results to that of traditional media coverage, especially for consumer-focused campaigns, the process can be quite different, and the rules are often hazy.

1. **What is the history of influencers?** Marketing and advertising pros have long since tapped influencers as spokespeople for brands dating back to the Queen and the Pope promoting the use of general medicine to common people. The concept of a digital influencer, however, has only become popular in recent years and it's still developing.

2. **What qualifies someone as a digital influencer is up for interpretation.** Is it the number of followers? Anyone can buy those. Level of engagement? That's all relative to their follower count. Is it quality of content shared? Yeah, that seems important. But the truth is there is no industry standard saying who can or can't be an official digital influencer. There is no professional society of influencers, no set of ethical standards to abide by and, because there isn't a ton of information out about influencers and their results, there's no set pricing structure or market for advertising or working with them. In 2019, the FCC put regulations into place requiring influencers to disclose any endorsements with #ad, although, this is rarely regulated.

3. **The cost of working with influencers can vary greatly from person to person.** Some may only request a trade for product or services, while others always require payment. It's important to remember that just like traditional media, influencers are dedicating their time and efforts to generate

content and they expect to eventually monetize what they are doing.

4. **Start with the end goal.** Once we understand that influencers don't have set standards for how they work with brands or even set pricing, how can you know what to expect from them and the best way to get results that help your bottom line? It all boils down to strategy and budget.

5. **As with traditional media and public relations, always start with the story and the audience you are trying to reach.** Dig deep into what you want to convey and then match that goal with a relevant publication or target outlet. The process is similar for influencers because many influencers focus on very specific subjects, so we are able to directly reach people interested in those topics through strategic targeting.

6. **When it comes to budget, be realistic.** These days almost any influencer worth their salt is charging or expecting something in return for sharing content so a budget should always be set aside for influencer payments. Pricing can vary greatly and there is no set science to knowing if a specific partnership will work, but we advise clients to be flexible with budget and understand that part of influencer marketing is trial and error. With so many algorithms and other factors at play on social media, it can be difficult to pinpoint when is exactly the best time, message, etc. to post for an influencer.

7. **Negotiate a budget and deliverables in advance – and don't forget to get it in writing!** The positive side to the chaos is everything is negotiable. In a good partnership, the influencer will want your team to see results, so you want to work with them again and again. Select partners who will allow you to tweak messaging or change the timing of posts to improve results and get confirmation that they will do this in writing –

but also give them the freedom to make creative decisions they know their audience will respond to best.

8. **Although it may seem like the Wild Wild West when it comes to digital influencers right now, in some ways it's not all that different from a traditional public relations and marketing approach.** Starting with the end goal in mind and developing a strategy around that is the first step to establishing a mutually beneficial relationship that earns you results.

TAKE ACTION: Review existing influencer partnership contracts for clarity in expectations and deliverables. If you don't have an existing contract, create a template that can be customized for future partners. Contracts should include expected content, timing of posts, compensation and all other guidelines and expectations for both the influencer and the hiring brand. Download an example contract:
www.reedpublicrelations.com/millennialsguide.

See Also:
Challenge 15: Working With Media (Do's and Don'ts)
Challenge 21: Finding Micro-Influencers to Fit Your Niche
Challenge 38: Knowing When a Celebrity Partnership is the Right Choice
Challenge 54: Practicing Ethical Marketing

Challenge 20: Finding the Right Content Creators for Your Brand

Because there's no specific guidelines or code of ethics for digital influencers, a brand partnership can result in great coverage, really awful coverage, or something in between. Influencers should be vetted and evaluated just as any other potential business partner or agency would be.

1. **Start by looking at hashtags.** If you are starting from scratch, look for creators using relevant hashtags for your brand and in your service area. For example, if you're a Nashville restaurant looking for a micro-influencer to dine in and post about your food, start with #nashville. You can refine your search from there — for example, try #nashvillefood, #nashvillefoodie, #nashvilleeats, #nashvilledinner. Scroll through the populated images and develop a list of potential influencers from there.

2. **Look at their voice and positioning.** Start by reviewing your website and marketing collateral. Is there a casual, conversational tone or is it more formal? Make sure the influencer you partner with is comfortable using the style of language your brand employs. This is critical to ensure posts about your organization or product are a natural fit on the feed. Content that's overtly "sales-y" leads to minimal engagement.

3. **Does the influencer's aesthetic match the brand's aesthetic?** You can pull directly from your brand standards to determine your organization's aesthetic. Do you use punchy, in-your-face colors and graphics? Or do you stick with a neutral palette? Influencers spend a lot of time and energy curating their feed's aesthetic. You won't have much luck asking an

influencer who posts all black-and-white images to promote your brightly colored product.

4. **Does the influencer's following reach your target demographic?** Look at who is following each influencer. Read comments on feed posts to get a sense of who's engaging with their content and why. An influencer's age can be a good indicator of the type of follower he or she attracts. It will also help to review previous brand partnerships and the types of products this individual has successfully promoted.

TAKE ACTION: Develop a list of 10 to 15 influencers that might be a fit for your organization. Examine each through the lenses outlined above and select those that are a fit to be a part of your next influencer campaign.

See Also:
Challenge 8: Determining Target Audiences
Challenge 18: Knowing What Platforms to Use
Challenge: 19: Working With Content Creators for Your Brand
Challenge 38: Knowing When a Celebrity Partnership is the Right Choice

Challenge 21: Finding Micro-Influencers to Fit Your Niche

When it comes to working with influencers such as bloggers, celebrities, and other social media personalities, sometimes less is more in terms of followers. You can easily spend hundreds or thousands of dollars for a single sponsored post from big-name influencers. Studies show that as an influencer's number of followers increases, their audience engagement decreases. Cue: the micro-influencer.

1. **Individuals with between 1,000 and 10,000 followers – known as micro-influencers – hold more power in today's digital world.** These micro-influencers tend to have a more engaged, loyal following. They are more likely to be seen as a trustworthy source of information and recommendations than influencers with hundreds of thousands or millions of followers. They are also usually more open to sharing posts in exchange for goods and services rather than monetary exchanges so they can be a cost-effective in that way as well.

2. **With each passing year, influencer trends shift dramatically, too.** The of-the-moment Instagram star is the micro-influencer, a social media personality with a small but highly engaged following. Every follower is part of a community and has chosen to be there. Followers are either highly interested in the topic the micro-influencer covers or strongly invested in the influencer's life. Compare this to celebrity influencers with 1MM+ followers—the influencer-follower connection isn't as strong.

3. **Consider micro-influencers for niche topics.** Increased engagement, authentic content and trust amongst followers make micro-influencers an excellent choice for brand partnerships They can also be regular people sharing a glimpse of their daily lives. Micro-influencers are cost-effective due to their smaller followings, but most importantly, they're often easy to work with and willing to share content that suits both parties.

4. **So, how do you go about finding the right micro-influencer for your brand? Start with hashtags.** Hashtags are the best method for influencer discovery. Start with general queries. For example, if you're a Nashville restaurant looking for a micro-influencer to dine in and post about your food, start with #nashville. You can refine your search from there—for example, try #nashvillefood, #nashvillefoodie, #nashvilleeats, #nashvilledinner. Scroll through the populated images and develop a list of potential micro-influencers for your partnership.

5. **Provide a brief and then let them do their thing.** Most influencers have built their followings organically and know what type of content resonates with their audiences. While you always want to provide a contract brief that outlines expectations and deliverables, it's also important to let them have the creative freedom to produce something engaging and attention-grabbing.

6. **Decide how you will measure success for your micro-influencer campaigns.** Setting metrics for measurement before your influencer program starts is key. Consider what your KPIs are and which metrics you will track that align with them.

TAKE ACTION: Identify 5 or 6 local micro-influencers that could be utilized for your next campaign. Follow them on Instagram (or their preferred platform) to get to know their style and level of follower engagement.

See Also:
Challenge 8: Determining Target Audiences
Challenge 18: Knowing What Platforms to Use
Challenge: 19: Working with Content Creators for Your Brand
Challenge 36: Knowing When a Celebrity Partnership is the Right Choice

Section 4: Digital Marketing

The divide between digital and traditional marketing is breaking down, and separate disciplines are now being viewed as one.

Challenge 22: Defining Digital Marketing

Digital marketing can be difficult to grasp because it encompasses so much. It essentially refers to any marketing outreach made via a computer, tablet, or mobile device – that's anything online including websites, search engine optimization and paid search results, blogs, video, email and social media.

1. **A brand's digital locale depends on their industry and needs.** A fast-food mogul like McDonald's may focus sharing creative, fun videos and working with online influencers while a mid-sized senior living community might prioritize curating client reviews and posting educational pieces on Facebook. There is no one-size-fits-all in digital marketing, and putting together the most effective strategies and tactics is half the fun.

2. **Digital is essential.** Your brand has a digital presence whether you are investing in digital marketing or not. Consumers leave reviews, talk on social media and can even register a business on sites like Google My Business and Yelp without actually owning the location (side note: go claim your Google My Business and Yelp pages!). Investing in digital marketing helps you drive the conversation and capture those leads.

3. **A bigger budget won't replace knowing your customer and message.** You can employ dozens of digital marketing tactics – SEO, Pay-Per-Click (PPC), email marketing, native advertising, social media – but none of them will be effective without having detailed knowledge about who you are targeting and what your message is.

4. **Use a SWOT analysis to guide your strategy.** A SWOT analysis identifies a brand's existing Strengths, Weaknesses, Opportunities and Threats. The results of a SWOT analysis can provide a framework for your digital marketing strategy. It can be helpful to conduct a SWOT analysis each year to reassess your progress and update your marketing tactics.

5. **Developing a digital media strategy involves looking at how short-term tactics can lead to long-term results.** Per the American Marketing Association, follow these basic steps to get started[8]:
   - **Identify Marketing Goals** – The first step in this process involves identifying specific goals, such as driving sales, generating leads, building brand recognition or increasing subscribers.
   - **Solidify Sales Process** – To maximize the benefits of digital marketing, it is necessary to understand the digital sales process and exactly how customers will make digital purchases.
   - **Isolate Target Customers** – Creating a strong target demographic with refined buyer personas helps isolate the ideal customers to purchase business goods or services.
   - **Choose Marketing Channels** – Armed with target demographic and buyer personas, it is important to identify the best digital marketing channels to reach those ideal customers.
   - **Set Clear Benchmarks** – In order to evaluate a digital marketing strategy, it is advisable to establish clear benchmarks for success and measure progress along the way.
   - **Make Necessary Adjustments** – After creating and implementing a digital marketing strategy, it is important to monitor progress toward goals and adjust as needed.

TAKE ACTION: Conduct a SWOT analysis of your organization and use the results to create a new digital marketing plan or revise an existing plan.

See Also:
Challenge 6: Be S.M.A.R.T! Setting Measurable Goals and Objectives
Challenge 19: Working With Content Creators & Influencers (Do's and Don'ts)
Challenge 55: Pursuing Measurable Results

Challenge 23: Creating an Effective Landing Page

A landing page gives your audience somewhere to learn more once they've engaged with your brand somewhere in the digital space. Whether they've clicked on a Google ad or followed a link in a company email, you want to hold that person's attention and push them further into the sales funnel with an effective landing page.

1. **Landing pages focus on long-term, qualified leads.** While you may employ several inbound marketing tactics, a well-designed landing page is one of the most effective in turning visitors into customers.

2. **Dial into a single goal.** A brand's main website will have multiple sections and pages for visitors to explore and get to know the products or services being offered. A landing page should focus on achieving one particular action from its visitors. Figuring out what your call-to-action should be depends on your overall marketing goals. It could be to have visitors sign up for a mailing list, RSVP to an event, schedule a consultation, register for a trial or make a purchase with a discount code.

3. **Streamline data collection.** Utilize tools that automatically transfer a user's information from a landing page's contact form into a spreadsheet. Most form-building applications have this option and it will make retargeting your audiences much easier later on.

4. **Keep communication going.** A landing page should be the beginning of a relationship with a customer, not the end. Once a visitor completes the call-to-action on your landing

page, determine what the best follow-up should be, whether it's an email campaign, retargeting through ads (this will take some coordinating with your webmaster and social media managers) or sending a mailed marketing piece as your next touchpoint.

TAKE ACTION: Brainstorm a marketing initiative or choose one from your existing marketing plan that can be improved by creating a landing page. Write out 3-4 bullet points about how the landing page will garner leads and how you will reach out to those leads once you've collected their information on the landing page.

See Also:
Challenge 5: I Have My Message! What's Next?
Challenge 24: Website Layout / Design
Challenge 56: Implementing Tools to Measure Your Success

Challenge 24: Website Layout / Design

It's no secret that a professional website is essential for any business or organization, but the nuances of a site's design can either help or hinder your marketing efforts. SEO (search engine optimization), is a highly effective tool for driving web traffic, gaining new clients and ultimately increasing revenue, but it has to be done right and in conjunction with good site design to be the most effective.

1. **You don't have to be a computer whiz to understand the basics of UX/UI design.** You can (and should) trust a skilled expert when it comes to your site's User Experience and User Interface, but you also need a basic understanding of these terms to help guide them. UX refers to a site's ease-of-use while UI is more about how a site looks visually. Both pieces start with knowing what your consumer's goals are when they visit your site. From there, you can build out intuitive navigation, clear paths to relevant information and easy-to-use applications, all supported by consistent branding.

2. **Make your website mobile-friendly to rank higher on Google.** Of course, you want your website to be mobile-friendly for the best user experience, but your mobile presence also affects your site's ranking on search engines. The algorithms behind Google and Bing prioritize sites with faster mobile page load speeds and will move a site higher on the list if it loads more quickly than other results.

3. **Dedicate an hour a week to SEO.** Building up your SEO is a continual process. Consider drafting and publishing case studies to show off your work with past clients, blog regularly about content relevant to your audience and continuously look

for ways to integrate keywords and phrases your customer's might be searching for.

4. **Build up your backlinks by sharing media coverage.** When your organization receives media attention, share the coverage on your website and link back to the original story by the publication. External links to your website (as are often included in media stories) are widely considered to be the most important source of ranking power for a website. Backlinks act as a signal to search engines that others vouch for your content, hence why they are highly valuable. Always work with your PR team to share major hiring announcements, new client acquisitions and office moves or expansions to capitalize on this SEO tactic.

TAKE ACTION: Make a list of keywords you imagine customers might be searching for. You can use tools like Keywordtool.io and Google Trends to help develop your list. Then, comb through your website and adjust verbiage to match the identified phrases exactly. Whenever possible, try to use the full phrase or sentence without being redundant. Make sure you're only including these words and phrases in places that make sense.

See Also:
Challenge 9: Communications Audit
Challenge 40: Starting Your Own Podcast
Challenge 45: Understanding Your Workplace Culture

Challenge 25: Marketing in the Metaverse

Here's the latest buzzword for you: metaverse. Since Facebook's acquisition of Oculus – one of the largest manufacturers of virtual reality headsets in the world – and their ultimate re-brand as "Meta" in 2021, there's been a lot of chatter about how companies will shift their digital marketing strategies to meet consumers in the virtual world.

While Meta has since pivoted their all-in approach on virtual reality to a more broad exploration of immersive tech, these virtual platforms are only expected to grow as a hotbed for reaching and interacting with consumers over the next decade.

But in a digital space where literally anything is possible, how do you know where to start?

1. **What (or where) is the metaverse?** Metaverse is a broad term. It isn't one centralized place – yet. Instead, it's a collection of digital worlds that allows users to work, play, socialize and shop just as they would in the physical world. It doesn't necessarily include virtual or augmented reality, although it can. For brands, it's a new frontier for marketing with opportunities for unique customer interactions that wouldn't be possible in the real world.

2. **Why market in the metaverse?** For starters, the metaverse is slated to become an $800 billion global market by 2024[9]. The largest population segment in the metaverse is Gen Z and they have major purchasing power. Bloomberg estimates Zillennials in the U.S. have $360 billion in disposable income as of 2021,[10] and they tend to value virtual items as much, if not more, than physical items. Think custom clothes for a virtual avatar or a limited

edition banner that shows they attended an exclusive online event. This is a stark contrast from older consumers that expect a physical item for their dollars and presents a potential new revenue stream for brands.

3. **The metaverse is still in its infancy.** Marketing in the metaverse requires some trial and error. You may even consider launching a "burner brand" – a pseudo company used to work out the kinks of a new campaign or platform – to test creative activations before launching with your official brand. The metaverse is still very new, so brands wanting to experiment in this new frontier need to be open-minded and willing to adapt as the technology changes. Over the next decade, we will see how individualized worlds come together to create a unified experience for consumers.

4. **Gamification promotions lead metaverse marketing tactics.** There's a subgroup of people who have been operating in the metaverse for years – gamers. As consumer brands consider how to engage with customers in a digital space, many companies are using concepts that have already proven successful within the gaming community. For example, Chipotle made waves by creating the first virtual restaurant in Roblox in 2021 that allowed customers complete in-game tasks like grilling ingredients and rolling virtual burritos to earn real-life rewards, such as a free entree. This is just one example of how "gamifying" a promotion can be used to create effective interactions with customers in the metaverse.

5. **Metaverse marketing should still be integrated marketing.** This is a new avenue, but the same rules apply. As you develop fun metaverse concepts, refer back to your brand values and overall marketing goals to ensure everything is in alignment. Identify what metrics are most important and

utilize public relations and social media to encourage engagement on your selected metaverse platform(s). Brands entering the metaverse are seen as innovative and future-forward, so take advantage by working that messaging into other areas of your marketing plan.

TAKE ACTION: Imagine you have an endless budget to create a virtual world for your target customers. Brainstorm 2-3 creative "gamified" activations you could implement to engage consumers in a digital space. Is there crossover with real-world items or services? What metrics would you use to measure success?

See Also:
Challenge 6: Be S.M.A.R.T! Setting Measurable Goals and Objectives
Challenge 18: Knowing What Platforms to Use
Challenge 20: Finding the Right Content Creators for Your Brand

Challenge 26: Integrating AI Into Your Marketing

Artificial Intelligence (AI) tools have transformed marketing and business operations overall. When OpenAI introduced ChatGPT to the world in November 2022, the chatbot garnered more than one million users in just five days. AI tools

1. **Types of AI for marketing.** AI encompasses more than just chatbots like ChatGPT. ChatGPT and other generative language tools like Bard by Google and Claude utilize AI to interact with human users in an almost human manner. They can be used to create content such as blog posts, social media posts, emails and more or to automate customer service tasks by responding to inquiries quickly and accurately.

   Outside of generative language tools, you also have generative image and video tools, such as Midjourney and Synthesia, as well as predictive AI tools, such as Tableau and Pecan AI, can analyze data to help marketers better understand and predict the outcomes of their campaigns. As AI grows and evolves, many existing CRMs are integrating AI into their systems, such as HubSpot's ChatSpot.ai tool and Salesforce's Einstein GPT software.

2. **Quality prompts will generate quality outputs.** With any generative AI tool – that is a tool that generates some form of content in the form of copy, images or videos – the key to getting results you can actually use is better prompting. Crafting the perfect prompt can be time consuming, but a few tips include defining the AI's role ("Act as a social media manager"), define who the target audience is and provide any additional context that will help it produce the best response possible.

ChatGPT Prompt Formula

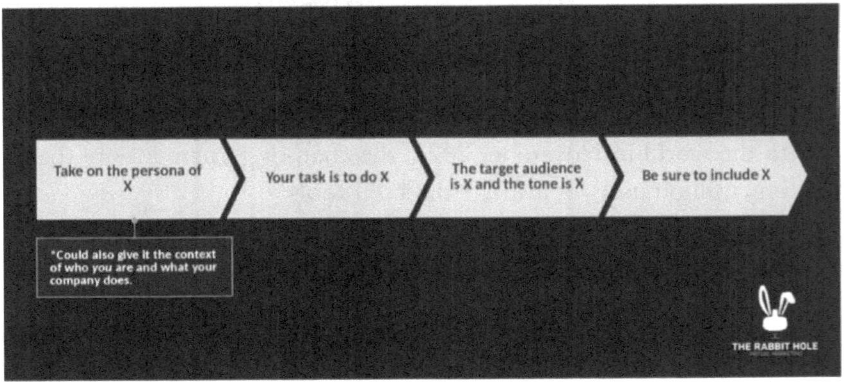

3. **Understand the pitfalls and limitations.** While there are many advantages of using AI in marketing campaigns, the technology isn't perfect yet. One common issue is privacy and data storage. If you are using a tool like ChatGPT, be careful not to divulge confidential company information as any inputs are stored and used to train the tool to produce better outputs. With AI-powered chatbots, companies must ensure they comply with relevant laws and regulations as the bots collect data from conversations with customers.

   Additionally, AI is known to experience "hallucinations," which is just a fancy way of saying they will make up an answer for you even if they don't know the true answer – and they are very convincing when they do it. To mitigate these risks, be sure to always review the content your AI tool produces, especially when it comes to exact numbers and percentages, to ensure accuracy.

4. **AI is evolving at breakneck speeds.** Even though AI has been in development for decades, it's only now being widely adopted by the general public because of consumer-friendly

interfaces like ChatGPT. Over the next few years, AI will continue to rapidly develop and change nearly every facet of our lives and our businesses. Marketers and business owners alike should adopt a learning mindset and make an intentional effort to continuously educate themselves about the latest technologies and techniques.

5. **Now you may be asking was this section written by ChatGPT? Was this entire book written by ChatGPT?!** The answer is no to both. While these tools can be valuable resources for outlining and planning, they are no substitution for real human expertise based on experience. As you develop content for your brand or your clients, remember to infuse your own knowledge to provide value to your audiences. And in a world where content will eventually be dominated by AI-produced pieces, stand out from the crowd by focusing on things that AI can't yet replicate such as podcasts and videos.

TAKE ACTION: Audit your current marketing strategies and identifying areas where AI tools like ChatGPT could enhance efficiency or creativity. Could you generate more creative social media content? Can you automate your email marketing campaigns? Then, research plugins for ChatGPT and consider how they could streamline these workflows. Have ChatGPT create an implementation plan to help get you started with integrating AI into your marketing.

See Also:
Challenge 32: Defining Thought Leadership
Challenge 40: Starting Your Own Podcast
Challenge 54: Practicing Ethical Marketing

Section 5: Event Management and Planning

Events allow the public to interact with a brand in a way that other marketing tactics can't. Some events are geared toward collecting data from leads and showcasing your service or product in the best light while others focus on generating goodwill within a community or simply raising brand awareness. Regardless of the goal, an event should aim to make a meaningful connection with your target audience.

Challenge 27: Event Planning (Do's and Don'ts)

Events are often cited as the reason young professionals want to work in PR and marketing, but it's not all free food and celebrity photo ops. Successful events take a lot of meticulous planning, and sometimes the most effective events aren't flashy or over-the-top but intimate and engaging.

1. **Assess event opportunities based on brand-fit.** The list of event opportunities is nearly endless from physical events like trade shows, conferences, ribbon-cuttings and open houses to virtual events such as webinars and livestreaming on social media. When considering where to have a presence, look at the cost and manpower required, identify the audience you plan to reach and set an event goal, whether that is to collect a certain number of qualified leads, increase visitors to your website with a scannable QR code, raise a certain amount of a money for a cause, etc. Event goals should be concrete and align with your brand and overarching marketing plan.

2. **Come with a timeline and a task list.** The key to a perfectly orchestrated event is preparation. During planning stages, develop a run-of-show document that outlines each major activity in an hour-by-hour timeline. Determine what particular actions need to be taken for each activity and by whom. Review your run-of-show days in advance to ensure all materials have been ordered or assembled and each task has been assigned to a team member.

3. **Gather your materials and your team.** What do you need to execute tactics on-site? Do certain items need to be ordered in advance to allow time for delivery or assembly?

If attending an event at a convention center or event hall, connect with their event management team for details on loading dock usage, electrical hookups and signage restrictions. Include these details in your run-of-show and make sure everyone has the latest copy on the day of the event.

4. **Develop a budget.** Include the cost of materials, external contractors such as photographers or videographers and other out-of-pocket costs for things like transportation, food and promotional takeaways. Adjustments can be made during an event, but funding should be estimated as closely as possible in the initial plan.

5. **Be nimble.** A few hiccups can always be expected regardless of how much you prepare, and event managers will need to think quickly and creatively to come to a solution. Sometimes you just need to keep things moving to stay on track with your event timeline. Other times, you may be presented with a great opportunity you weren't expecting, like a media interview with a major publication. You want to stay nimble and adaptable regardless of the situation. Always refer to your event goal and think about what will help you achieve it.

6. **Re-consider event sponsorship without any other form of engagement.** People are inundated with images and information at events, so having your logo on the brochure may or may not be an effective use of funds. It can generate goodwill with a particular organization – and sometimes that is enough to be worthwhile – but in general you will also want to engage attendees in some way to get the most bang for your buck.

7. **Evaluate after each event.** As with any marketing tactic, events should have metrics by which to measure success. In your evaluation, compare actual expenses to initial budget estimates, assess if quantifiable goals were met (number of leads collected, media interviews secured, etc.) and make notes about what went well and how future events can be improved.

TAKE ACTION: Create a template for a run-of-show document. Include a timeline format that is easy to follow and update, special activities (giveaways, contest drawings, pre-scheduled media interviews, etc.) and team members responsible for each piece. You may also include a section for special guests with names, titles, and headshots so your team can recognize and greet them appropriately.

See Also:
Challenge 12: Creating an Effective Media List
Challenge 13: Writing Compelling Pitches & Press Releases
Challenge 28: Don't Forget the Big Scissors… (How to Plan the Perfect Grand Opening)
Challenge 30: Thinking Outside the Box

Challenge 28: Don't Forget the Big Scissors. (How to Plan the Perfect Grand Opening)

A grand opening is more than just an event – it's an experience. It's an opportunity to show the market who you are and set the standard for years to come.

1. **Draw people in.** Consider what will entice people to attend your grand opening. Refreshments, product demos, behind-the-scenes tours and special pricing are all ways to get butts in seats while making an impression. Spread the word with a grand opening press release, social media announcements and email blasts with details about what to expect.

2. **Combine traditional and digital marketing tactics.** A ribbon-cutting is still a great ceremonial photo op at a grand opening, but modern events should combine traditional outreach to media outlets, local officials and partner organizations as well as embrace digital tactics like utilizing custom QR codes to drive traffic to a landing page, inviting bloggers and social media influencers to attend or simply collecting emails from attendees.

3. **As the budget allows, implement creative ideas that linger well after the event is over.** This could be a traditional takeaway swag bag, sending discount codes to folks who provided their emails at the event or something more interactive like a photo booth where guests take branded pictures and share to social media. Don't forget to display the event hashtag and the brand's

social handle so you can measure social reach in your post-event evaluation. The goal is to keep the buzz going with your audience after the event has wrapped.

4. **Have a designated spokesperson ready to go.** Most grand openings will have a speaker or two say a few words. Include when they are speaking on your run-of-show and prep them with talking points ahead of time. If the speaker is from outside of your organization, talk with them about what will be said beforehand. At least one spokesperson from your organization should be media trained and prepared for interviews on-site.

5. **Put together a timetable and a task list.** Who is responsible for making sure each task is accomplished both before and during the event? Develop a run-of-show document that outlines each major activity in an hour-by-hour timeline. Determine what particular actions need to be taken for each activity and by whom. Review your run-of-show days in advance to ensure all materials have been ordered or assembled and each task has been assigned to a team member.

6. **Develop a budget.** Include the cost of materials, external contractors such as photographers or videographers and other out-of-pocket costs for things like transportation, food, florals and promotional takeaways. Adjustments can always be made leading up to an event, but funding should be estimated as closely as possible in the initial plan.

7. **Set metrics for evaluation on the frontend.** How will you determine if you are reaching your objectives? What will

you measure or observe, and how will you do that? Who will be responsible for assembling the postmortem report? Starting with the end goal in mind will prime your event for success.

TAKE ACTION: Brainstorm 2 to 3 creative ideas to execute at your next grand opening event that will keep your organization top-of-mind after the event is over.

See Also:
Challenge 12: Creating an Effective Media List
Challenge 13: Writing Compelling Pitches & Press Releases
Challenge 29: Pivot! How to Adjust When Things Go Wrong
Challenge 31: Thinking Outside the Box

Challenge 29: Pivot! How to Adjust When Things Go Wrong

A few hiccups can be expected at any event. Preparation and adaptability are essential for course-correcting when things don't go as planned. There is always a solution if you can keep level-headed and focused on the end goal.

1. **Be nimble.** Event managers have to think quickly and creatively to find a solution when things go awry. Sometimes you just need to keep things moving to stay on track with your event timeline. Other times, you may be presented with an unexpected opportunity, like a media interview with a major publication, that you want to take advantage of. Stay nimble and adaptable regardless of the situation and refer back to your goals to determine what to do next.

2. **Identify the local shipping centers, print shops and supply stores.** Forgot nametags? There's an Office Depot® around the corner. The poster you ordered online didn't arrive in time? Email it to the nearest FedEx® and call about having the printing expedited for pickup. Familiarizing yourself with your on-the-ground resources will allow you to move quickly if an issue arises.

3. **Have a rain plan.** Or a pandemic plan or a natural disaster plan. Sometimes things are outside of our control, but we can think through the possibilities and have a few options waiting in the wings. This could be as simple as moving an event inside due to bad weather or taking an in-person seminar virtual due to illness.

4. **Attitude and communication are everything.** Train your team on what to do and how to act professionally when things go

wrong. Rely on each other rather than place blame in the moment. You can always look at issues more closely during your event evaluation to determine what happened and what can be done to keep it from happening again.

TAKE ACTION: Create a contact sheet for your internal events team. Make sure everyone's direct lines and cell phone numbers are listed. If you've had new team members join or past team members leave, update the list accordingly. Share the final version with the team.

See Also:
Challenge 28: Don't Forget the Big Scissors… (How to Plan the Perfect Grand Opening)
Challenge 44: Establishing Effective Internal Communications Channels
Challenge 47: Proactive Risk Management

Challenge 30: Event Activations

Event activations – or brand activations – are an experiential marketing tactic meant to engage a specific target audience. They are usually one-off events that offer creative ways for people to interact with a brand. Think about the Oscar Mayer™ Wienermobile handing out free hotdogs at a pet adoption event or DIRECTV® hosting a game viewing party with a VIP experience for select attendees. Event activations take a lot of different forms, but the end goal is all the same: connect with your audience to create a meaningful bond between brand and consumer.

1. **Identify a target audience and where they will be.** Event activations work best when they engage a specific population segment. Identify the groups you want to build a deeper connection with as a brand. These target audience(s) should be clearly defined and grouped together by what they have in common.

2. **Include an element of surprise.** A little surprise-and-delight goes a long way to get people talking. Whether it's a large-scale installation of some sort or a pop-up with unexpected goodies, get your audience excited with a fun surprise that aligns with your core values and overarching marketing message.

3. **Event activations should be fun, but they also have to be effective.** Investing time and money into an activation that is misguided or under-representing the brand is a waste. So while you want to be creative and innovative, it still has to make sense from a business perspective. If your audience remembers the stunt but not the brand behind it, there's been a misstep.

4. **Research past event activations for inspiration.** Global companies like KFC® and Nike® have implemented some of the best event activations in history – some with positive feedback and others that either fell flat or resulted in backlash. Look into campaigns from big brands such as these for both inspiration and words of warning.

TAKE ACTION: Review the list of events you are already planning to attend this year or next. Brainstorm an exciting event activation for at least two of them that goes beyond a typical marketing event to engage and illicit a response from consumers.

See Also:
Challenge 13: Writing Compelling Pitches & Press Releases
Challenge 28: Don't Forget the Big Scissors… (How to Plan the Perfect Grand Opening)
Challenge 31: Thinking Outside the Box
Challenge 36: Finding a Cause That Aligns With Your Brand

Challenge 31: Thinking Outside the Box

When you are running PR and marketing campaigns all the time, it's easy to get tied to what you know works. But strategies and tactics need to evolve with the times and be tailormade for the specific project being promoted. Particularly in a post-pandemic world, marketers need to think creatively about how to reach their audiences and leave a lasting impression.

1. **Start with a crazy, no holds barred idea and work backward from there.** In an initial brainstorming session, don't limit yourself to a budget or even necessarily what's realistic. Throw out the biggest, most outlandish ideas then pare them down to get to a concept that's actually feasible. For example, if you are promoting the opening of a ski resort, you may want to bring in live penguins to slide down the bunny slopes for the media. That may not be possible, so instead you opt for setting up snow-making machines in hotspots around the city, making it snow to capture the attention of locals and tourists alike. This brainstorming technique will keep you from self-limiting and promote creative thinking.

2. **Look at other industries and brainstorm ways to apply their tactics within your organization.** Sometimes we get trapped in what is standard for the restaurant industry or healthcare industry or beauty industry. Research brands making waves in industries that have nothing to do with your product or service. What is spiking engagement and how can it be customized as a creative solution for your campaign?

3. **Separate yourself from competitors.** Go where your competitors aren't and look for unexpected avenues that will set you apart. For example, most companies like to send client gifts and cards around Christmas time, but could you get noticed more if you

sent a New Year's gift or a Christmas in July card instead? Identify your differentiator and think about how to show it off in a unique way so you don't get lost in the shuffle.

4. **Out-of-the-box ideas still need to align with your brand's core values and marketing messages.** Develop brand filters that will serve as a litmus test to run ALL communications through to ensure your marketing message doesn't drift, regardless of how creative or innovative an idea is.

5. **Virtual events can be engaging and interactive.** For the safety of your audience, sometimes you have to go virtual. When you have to skip in-person events you would regularly attend, consider hosting webinars and informational sessions on Zoom. The one positive side to the pandemic has been the widespread adoption of online meeting services, so it shouldn't be difficult to find attendees. Remember all the same principles still apply: set your marketing goal for the event, be engaging and measure success afterward.

TAKE ACTION: Host an idea dump session with your team. Give a brief overview of the project and set a timer for five minutes to jot down as many creative ideas as possible. When the time is up, have everyone share their ideas aloud. These won't be fully fleshed out thoughts, but they can serve as a starting point for a bigger vision. Sometimes several ideas can be coupled together to create one really great idea.

See Also:
Challenge 21: Finding Micro-Influencers to Fit Your Niche
Challenge 30: Event Activations
Challenge 37: Implementing Cause Marketing Campaigns
Challenge 42: Attending Trade Shows

Section 6: Credibility and Brand Reputation

For both B2C and B2B businesses, there's one thing that can set you apart from the competition: your expertise. Positioning your brand and team as subject-matter experts raises brand awareness and ultimately drives sales. The key is to build credibility over time by being a helpful resource for future clients rather than a pushy salesman who only enters the conversation when they can make a quick buck.

Challenge 32: Defining Thought Leadership

The words "thought leadership" get tossed around a lot in our industry, but few people understand what it means or how to achieve thought leadership status. Here's a secret: it's not that complicated. A thought leader is just that—someone who is a leader of thought in their industry or field. You must have expertise that people want to hear or read about. Those "thoughts" are usually niche, and you should have the skillset, degree or personal experience to back them up.

1. **Become an expert.** To become a thought leader, start with your expertise. Did you invent the internet? Engineer the first self-driving car? Create microwavable popcorn? It's OK if you didn't. You don't have to be the first to do something in your field to be considered an expert, but you do have to have the technical skills and knowledge to back up the advice you're dishing out. A PR and marketing team can help craft a brand message and get it noticed, but good thought leaders are able to bring real value and authenticity to their audiences.

2. **Be willing to advise.** Being a thought leader takes courage. Someone may want to be positioned as a thought leader but then get cold feet when the time comes for a thought leadership column to be published. Putting your expertise out into the world is a scary thing. You need to have confidence in yourself. You can't be a thought leader without voicing an opinion.

3. **If you are truly an expert, have quality content and establish a solid baseline of local coverage, you could be a thought leader!** It won't happen overnight, but when it does, establishing yourself as a thought leader in your industry can separate you

from the competition and help build trust with your audiences.

4. **Don't forget that thought leadership is just one component of an overarching communications campaign.** Whether establishing your expertise locally or working toward your next national feature, always be sure your thought leadership plan is strategic, measurable and aligns with the overall goals of your organization. With a little patience and a lot of perseverance, you'll soon be fielding calls from reporters reaching out to you for insights and comments!

TAKE ACTION: List 2 to 3 topics on which you or an executive at your organization could be a thought leader. Then list 2 to 3 opportunities such as thought leadership columns or speaking opportunities per topic that can be pursued within the next six months.

See Also:
Challenge 13: Writing Compelling Pitches & Press Releases
Challenge 15: Working With Media (Do's and Don'ts)
Challenge 40: Starting Your Own Podcast

Challenge 33: Why Thought Leadership (You're Already an Expert, So Why Not Share What You Know?)

In a world where companies are often faceless brands relentlessly pushing the next best thing, thought leadership gives you the opportunity to personalize your expertise and better connect with your audiences by being a resource for them. Crafting insightful, engaging content does take some time and energy, but if you're already a practiced expert in your field, it's as easy as talking about what you know.

1. **There are dozens of ways to share your expertise.** One reason to invest in thought leadership is you aren't tied to any one platform or content type. If you're a wordsmith, you might pen a bylined column for the local business journal whereas if you are a better public speaker, you might prefer to host a webinar or give a presentation to your regional trade association. Writing a blog, hosting a podcast, providing quotes for media stories and even a well-thought-out LinkedIn post are forms of thought leadership content.

2. **You can build trust with your audiences through thought leadership.** By giving them something of value and demonstrating your knowledge, you position yourself as a resource rather than a pushy salesman. That trust translates into increased sales. In fact, according to a study by LinkedIn and Edelman,[11] 60 percent of decision makers said thought leadership convinced them to buy a product or service they were not previously considering.

3. **Use your insights to generate leads.** Thought leadership is a great PR/media relations tool, but it can also be used to collect qualified leads via gated content. As an expert in your field,

you can put together a collateral piece – whether it be a guidebook, white paper, infographic or template – and require visitors to your landing page or website to complete a contact form to gain access. The result is a direct roster of people in need of your product or service.

4. **Stand out from the competition.** Spoiler alert: your competition may have some of the same skillsets that you do. But if you are better at positioning yourself as a thought leader to your ideal customer, the public and your peers, you can stand out as the more knowledgeable option. This, in turn, increases SEO, boost brand awareness and increases your chances of journalists reaching out to you for comment on future stories about your field.

5. **Thought leadership content is shareable.** When you've got something good, there's no need to recreate the wheel. A quality thought leadership piece can be shared and re-shared on social media, on the company blog, in e-newsletters and with your internal team.

TAKE ACTION: Assemble a suite of materials that can be used as gated content. This content can still be free but should require visitors to complete a contact form to access it.

See Also:
Challenge 4: Your Message Matters – How Do You Know You're on the Right Track?
Challenge 17: Growing Your Reach and Following
Challenge 34: Securing Op-Eds and Speaking Opportunities
Challenge 40: Starting Your Own Podcast

Challenge 34: Securing Op-Eds and Speaking Opportunities

Having the expertise to be a thought leader is one thing. Convincing media and other organizations to help you share that expertise is another. Op-ed columns and speaking engagements are two of the most valuable approaches to thought leadership because they require something that you can't produce yourself: third-party validation.

1. **Come with something to say.** Landing an op-ed or a speaking gig largely depends on if you have something of value to contribute. It can be helpful to pre-draft an op-ed piece and pitch it to a relevant media for consideration. Particularly if it is commenting on or providing educational context about a timely event, it's more likely to get picked up if an editor sees you have something ready to go.

2. **For speaking opportunities, research the speaker lineup from previous events** to get a feel for the type of content the organizers are looking for and the type of audience they attract. Tailor your pitch to feature a topic in line with their usual content while bringing something new to the table such as a fresh perspective and/or research data.

3. **Positioning will depend on placement.** A thought leadership column geared toward your ideal customer shouldn't be approached in the same way as a column geared toward your industry colleagues. Writing with a particular audience in mind can inform how you execute your column or presentation. Consider who you are targeting and position yourself as an expert to them accordingly.

4. **Put together a personal press kit.** You may already have a press kit for your organization at the ready with a company logo, backgrounder, and other marketing pieces, but the first ask from an editor placing an op-ed or on a speaker's application is typically for a personal bio and hi-res headshot. Assemble these items ahead of time to make submitting them for consideration easy.

5. **Lay a foundation with local media.** Once you're a subject matter expert and feel you have something valuable to contribute, that's when the magic can happen. Although it's not actually magic; there's a strategy behind it. A PR team or in-house PR manager should first work in your local market and with industry publications to establish credibility. In most cases, before landing *The New York Times,* you should start with the local daily or business publication. Any national reporter will immediately Google you if they receive a pitch and don't recognize your name. When they do, you want them to find positive articles and clips of you sharing your expertise on a local or regional level. A baseline of relevant, local coverage paired with a skilled pitch and a timely angle can be just enough to pique a national outlet's interest.

5. **Be willing to start small with speaking too.** With little to no prior speaking engagements on your resume, it will be difficult to book big conferences or conventions. Start by speaking to small community groups and local organizations. Hone your public speaking skills, and when you feel confident, film your next engagement. Use the footage to submit for bigger and better opportunities. With enough time and practice, events will start reaching out to you to speak at their events.

6. **Be patient. Keep trying.** The final piece of the equation is one of the toughest: patience. Once you have a solid hold on your local media market, a PR team should continue to develop

fresh angles and ideas to have your expertise included in bigger and bigger outlets. This might include tying your expertise into a current national trend or developing a column with a unique perspective. Securing an op-ed placement can happen quickly if the timing is right, but it typically takes weeks or even months for print publications that have long lead times. The key is patience and continual outreach to boost your chances of a national feature.

TAKE ACTION: Build out a thought leadership calendar. This could include relevant events with speaking opportunities, deadlines to submit for those opportunities, target publications for op-eds with links to their editorial calendars, and important dates throughout the year in case an op-ed topic is more timely around certain holidays or seasons.

See Also:
Challenge 8: Determining Target Audiences
Challenge 12: Creating an Effective Media List
Challenge 13: Writing Compelling Pitches & Press Releases
Challenge 33: Why Thought Leadership (You're Already an Expert, So Why Not Share What You Know?)

Section 7: Cause Marketing

Cause marketing is a collaboration between a for-profit business and a nonprofit organization for a common benefit. Today's cause marketing programs go beyond your standard community volunteering or corporate social responsibility initiative to engage consumers and employees for the greater good.

Challenge 35: Why Cause Marketing, You Ask?

It's the pair of shoes you bought because the brand guarantees a pair will be donated to a child in need. It's the hat you purchased because the brand advocates for nature conservation. It's the pink cookie you bought in October that supported breast cancer research (and because you like cookies). We're surrounded by cause marketing every day. Whether we realize it or not, it plays a huge role in our decision-making process as consumers.

1. **Consumers prefer purpose-driven brands.** Today's consumers expect brands to do more than just sell products; they want to support companies that give back to their communities. Millennials have always valued companies that do well by doing good, but Generation Z (those born 1997 and later) unequivocally demand it. Remaining neutral on hot-button issues is no longer an option[12]. As Gen Z takes over more and more of the consumer market, brands will need to get on board or get lost.

2. **Cause marketing benefits everyone involved.** When aligned with the right cause, brands can boost sales and community engagement by showing their customers they care about bettering society. Conversely, many nonprofits have a limited budget for marketing, and partnering with a brand can help get the word out about their efforts outside of their typical audiences. A successful cause marketing program benefits both parties and has a positive impact on the world.

3. **It's great for employee engagement and retention.** Millennials still make up the lion's share of the workforce while some of the oldest Gen Z-ers graduated from college

and entered the workforce in 2020. Combined, they are the most socially conscious generations and they are dominating the talent pool. To attract and retain top talent, brands should look to adopt an authentic cause marketing campaign that engages employees as well as consumers.

TAKE ACTION: Identify four or five causes (not specific organizations) that could be a genuine fit for your brand. Consider your ideal customer and what cause will resonate with them.

See Also:
Challenge 31: Thinking Outside the Box
Challenge 43: Developing an Employee Relations Plan
Challenge 51: Launching Successful Grassroots Campaigns
Challenge 54: Practicing Ethical Marketing

Challenge 36: Finding a Cause That Aligns With Your Brand

How do you win over consumers who are increasingly socially conscious? It starts with choosing the right non-profit partner. When brainstorming causes your brand could work with, consider what makes business sense and integrates seamlessly into your company culture.

1. **Start by answering these questions:**
   - Does the cause align with your brand? Do you share the same core values?
   - Does the cause resonate with your target consumers as well as your employees?
   - Does it alienate any of your key audiences?

2. **Once you have narrowed down potential non-profit partners with the initial questions, it's important to dig even deeper to make a final selection.**
   - Does the organization have a strong online/social presence with cross-promotional opportunities?
   - Is the organization actually interested in a true partnership with you?
   - How flexible is the organization in allowing you to customize the programs?
   - Is the organization efficient and responsible with its funding?
   - What is its overall reputation?
   - Do the core values and mission of the organization align with yours?
   - Is the organization large enough to cover your geographic reach and effectively cross-promote your brand?

- Is the organization of a size where you can truly make a difference and won't be among countless corporate partners?

3. **Coordinate with the non-profit before you launch.** Cause marketing should be a true partnership between the brand and the non-profit, so a representative from the non-profit should be involved from the start. As well-intentioned as it may be, you don't want to start a program claiming to benefit a non-profit without their knowledge. It will come across as disingenuous and it may even be illegal if they haven't authorized you to use their logos or slogans.

TAKE ACTION: Analyze any existing non-profit partnerships using the parameters above. If searching for a new non-profit partner, create a checklist from these questions and filter down candidates until you have 2 to 3 top choices.

See Also:
Challenge 8: Determining Target Audiences
Challenge 10: Developing Key Messages
Challenge 20: Finding the Right Content Creators for Your Brand
Challenge 45: Understanding Your Workplace Culture

Challenge 37: Implementing Cause Marketing Campaigns

Many small businesses might not have the budget to write a hefty check to a non-profit of their choice, and that's okay. Look at where your company currently stands financially and think of what your business can offer other than just money.

1. **Cause marketing is not philanthropy.** Philanthropy would be writing a check, sending it to a non-profit organization and sharing the news on the company Facebook page. Cause marketing is a much more in-depth process that involves spreading the word that a brand supports a particular cause, thus boosting sales for the brand and bringing more attention to the cause. Effective cause marketing typically involves more than just one campaign; it is an extensive program that permeates multiple parts of a brand's identity.

2. **It must be authentic.** It sounds easy enough—support a good cause, show the world your generosity and your sales will increase. But it's not enough for a brand to simply stand behind a cause and expect a return on investment. Both Millennials and Gen Z crave authenticity, and they are becoming more skeptical when it comes to brands supporting causes. They want to know the brand genuinely believes in what they stand for instead of leaning on corporate social responsibility to profit. If your campaign is not sincere, it will fail. The brand must live and breathe the values of the cause they are marketing or consumers won't buy it.

3. **It must engage both employees and consumers through an integrated campaign.** Your people on the frontlines are your best brand ambassadors. They need to understand the cause

and be passionate about it to encourage customers to support the mission as well.

4. **It must be measurable.** While supporting a cause is a worthwhile endeavor on its own, cause marketing does serve a business purpose. Cause marketing campaigns should be measurable just as any other marketing campaign would be. Depending on the tactics employed, each campaign might be evaluated based on social reach, media impressions, website traffic, consumer engagement and brand sentiment.

5. **Assess your cause marketing campaign with these filters:**
   - Does the cause make business sense?
   - Is it turnkey? Can it be efficiently executed by the team and resources you have available?
   - Does it resonate with your internal and external audiences?
   - Does it alienate any of your internal or external audiences?
   - What is the ROI?

TAKE ACTION: Outline a cause marketing plan for your chosen cause and partner organization. Set a goal and a timeline, provide an overview of tactics, propose a budget and list the metrics you will use to evaluate success.

See Also:
Challenge 6: Be S.M.A.R.T! Setting Measurable Goals and Objectives
Challenge 20: Finding the Right Content Creators for Your Brand
Challenge 42: Establishing Effective Internal Communication Channels
Challenge 55: Pursuing Measurable Results

Section 8: Celebrity Partnerships

Celebrity endorsements have long been a part of traditional marketing, dating back to the 1760s when Josiah Wedgwood, the founder of a pottery and chinaware company, employed royalty to endorse the quality and value of his products.[13] In the modern age, celebrity partnerships look a little different with social media influencers garnering just as much reach and credibility as Hollywood actors and political figures.

Challenge 38: Knowing When a Celebrity Partnership is the Right Choice

Having a celebrity represent your brand sounds like an easy marketing tactic, but shelling out celeb-level cash may not be the most efficient option to get results. On one hand, celebrities have fantastic reach and influence, but on the other hand, it can be easy to miss the mark if their following is too broad or their fame overshadows the product or service.

1. **Define "celebrity."** If you are approaching a major national or international star, you can expect a national or international price tag. As today's media landscape continues to change, so do the people who are telling brand stories. A local celebrity or influencer may be just as effective as a national name, if not more so, depending on the demographic you are trying to reach. Focus on the quality of their audience rather than quantity.

2. **If the photo op is essential, it could be worth it.** For events or destination promotions, a celebrity appearance and photo op could be worthwhile. Photos have staying power and can be used again and again as a future marketing piece. For individual product promotions or endorsements, you'll need to weigh the celebrity's following and engagement levels against the price per post to determine if it's the right choice.

3. **We want fame, not infamy.** Many a brand deal has been severed due to a celebrity's poor behavior. Not only could a celebrity's current reputation change, but you will want to do research into their past social media posts, appearances, and media clips to ensure they align with your organization's core values and would be a quality

representative of the brand. Regardless of how squeaky clean a celebrity may be, it is wise to have a response plan ready in case news breaks that they have been involved with something outside of your brand's values.

TAKE ACTION: Identify 1 to 2 local celebrities that could be a good fit for a partnership and request their media kits (if they have one). Then identify 1 to 2 more mainstream celebrities and reach out to their representing agency or manager about pricing per promotion. Compare the two and make a choice based on budget and the goals behind the celebrity partnership.

See Also:
Challenge 6: Be S.M.A.R.T! Setting Measurable Goals and Objectives
Challenge 19: Working With Content Creators & Influencers (Do's & Don'ts)
Challenge 21: Micro-Influencers to Fit Your Niche
Challenge 54: Practicing Ethical Marketing

Section 9: Traditional Advertising / Paid Media

When considering paid vs. earned media, marketers have to consider their budget, where their audiences are and how to cut through the noise to make an impression. The best marketing strategy is an integrated one and the only question is which area to put more emphasis on – not if you should do one or the other.

Challenge 39: Knowing When to Pursue Paid Opportunities

The days of a completely organic marketing campaign are gone. While producing organic content is still important for a well-rounded campaign, it can't necessarily stand on its own anymore and you will likely need to utilize some paid advertising to get noticed. The key is to strategically place your ad dollars, whether investing in traditional or digital advertising, to show up in the right places at the right time.

1. **Earned media has its perks, but it can be difficult to acquire.** Earned media refers to any content that does not provide compensation to the platform or outlet where it appears. The benefits include increased brand awareness, heightened credibility from being featured by an unpaid, reputable source and a boost in SEO as backlinks from credible websites prompt search engines to rank you higher. Plus, it doesn't require a monetary investment outside of the PR team securing the stories. But it takes time and effort to get noticed by journalists, and once you land coverage, it can be difficult – though not impossible – to translate the success into hard numbers.

2. **Paid media requires a bigger budget, but it's easy to secure.** As the name suggests, paid media includes any content that requires payment to be published such as sponsored content, advertorials and social media ads. In a matter of minutes, you can be running an Instagram ad targeted directly at your followers. However, digital ads take a special skillset to really be effective so you'll want to invest in a professional in addition to the money it will take to run the ads.

3. **You have more control with paid media.** Paid ads can be very specific in their content and placement. You don't have to worry about a writer editorializing a detail or getting the facts wrong. You choose the image, the copy, the audience and the timing. This can be especially helpful if you are promoting a

complex product or service. Paid media allows you to present your differentiators on your own terms and deliver it directly to the ideal customer.

4. **Organic reach on social media is nearly impossible.** Purely organic growth has become more difficult as most social media platforms have restructured to rely on paid ads as a primary revenue source. Modern algorithms prioritize paid content over everything else and can even hide your unpaid posts from your existing followers. You will almost certainly need to allocate part of your budget to social media advertising if social is part of your marketing plan.

5. **Paid digital ads are easily measurable.** Standard Pay-Per-Click ads like Google Ads (Formerly Google AdWords) and social media ads offer the benefit of analytics. You can data-mine your way through exactly how many times an ad was viewed, interacted with, by whom and the demographic info behind each user. On some platforms, you can see what day of the week and what time of day your ads perform the best and you can retarget and redistribute ads to users who have previously clicked or visited your website. This provides valuable insights into your customer base and marketing strategy.

TAKE ACTION: Consider your brand and make a pros and cons list for earned media and a second list for paid media. The list with more pros should take priority in your marketing plan.

See also:
Challenge 17: Growing Your Reach and Following
Challenge 22: Defining Digital Marketing
Challenge 38: Knowing When a Celebrity Partnership is the Right Choice
Challenge 55: Pursuing Measurable Results

Section 10: Podcasting

It seems like everyone has a podcast these days – and for good reason. Podcasts have brought audio-based media to the forefront of marketing when it has typically been reserved for radio in the past.

Challenge 40: Starting Your Own Podcast

The decision to start a podcast shouldn't be taken lightly as it does require some initial resources and an ongoing investment of time to develop into a successful marketing tool. If you can find your niche and audience, though, podcasts are a great way to reach listeners directly with your marketing messages.

1. **Identify your niche.** What is your expertise? Podcasts are a form of thought leadership, and good thought leaders can bring real value and authenticity to their audiences. Just as your brand has differentiators that separate it from the competition, you will need to identify your own personal differentiator and highlight it on the podcast.

2. **Keep it casual and conversational.** Some podcasts are made for entertainment, others for news. If you are utilizing a podcast for marketing purposes, there is no need to adopt a character personality or to be overly formal. Lean on your real personality to come across as authentic and knowledgeable in your field.

3. **Create an upload schedule – and stick to it.** This is one of the biggest downfalls for new podcasts. Listeners crave a consistent upload schedule, so they know when to expect new episodes of your show. Many listeners use podcasts to get through their daily commute, while they are eating lunch at work, every morning in the shower, etc. An ideal upload schedule is the same day each week or each month. Even if it is once per quarter, try to develop some consistency around when you will create new podcasts and when they will go live.

4. **Don't forget video.** Some of the most popular podcasts in the world aren't just listened to – they are watched on YouTube.

So, while the heart of your podcast is audio, it can be worth investing in a camera set-up and editing software to create a visual version as well. Podcasts on YouTube also have the potential to become passive revenue streams if you are uploading regularly and garnering a following.

TAKE ACTION: Make a list of items you need to get your podcast started. In addition to the physical equipment, include non-tangible items such as the suggested upload schedule, episode ideas, and how it will be promoted and used to market your overall brand.

See also:
Challenge 8: Determining Target Audiences
Chellenge 16: Developing Content & Telling a Compelling Story
Challenge 32: Defining Thought Leadership
Challenge 56: Implementing Tools to Measure Your Success

Challenge 41: Finding Your Audience and Growing Your Listenership

In 2021, there were about two million podcast shows for listeners to choose from, according to Podcast Insights. That number can seem daunting when you think about how to break into the podcast world starting at zero listeners. But the number of podcast listeners is just as impressive: 16 million people in the U.S. are "avid podcast fans" (Nielsen, 2018), and 50 percent of all U.S. homes are podcast fans (Nielsen, 2017).[14] With numbers like those, there's almost certainly a listenership for your podcast out there, but it will take a strategic approach to capture them.

1. **Treat your podcast like a company product.** Because that's what it is. To have a successful podcast, you should invest money in infrastructure, dedicate time and staffing and be willing to share your expertise with the world. Even though it is a marketing tool, it should be treated and marketed as a product itself. Identify who your audience is for the podcast and the channels you will use to get it in front of them. Studies show smart phone usage has contributed to the mass adoption of podcasts, so think through how your podcast will be distributed and how easy it is for a listener to access.

2. **Tap your existing "fans."** Getting you existing consumer base to follow and listen to your podcast is the low-hanging fruit. Put a link to the podcast in your email bio, announce it in your client newsletter and encourage your internal team to like and follow the podcast pages online. You could also invite some of your clients on as guests and encourage them to share their episode with their teams and followers. All these pieces will lead to a larger listenership over time.

3. **Go after new listeners who could benefit from your expertise.** Once you have a few episodes published and a reliable schedule of new content forthcoming, reach out to business organizations, relevant blogs or future clients and invite them to listen in. Emphasize the educational aspects of your podcast and explain that you thought they might find it useful. If your budget allows, you can also pursue new listeners with paid ads on social media targeting users with interests in your podcast topic.

TAKE ACTION: Create a podcast marketing plan. This should detail your niche, target audience, the topics of the first 3 to 5 episodes to be recorded before you launch and the strategies and tactics you will use to market the podcast.

See Also:
Challenge 8: Determining Target Audiences
Challenge 17: Growing Your Reach and Following
Challenge 40: Starting Your Own Podcast

Section 11: Product Launches

We live in a world of endless choices and the ability to get almost anything delivered to our doors in a matter of hours. To set a new product or service apart, marketers need to be in touch with where their ideal consumer is – in reality and digitally – and the best ways to reach them if they want to get noticed.

Challenge 42: Attending Trade Shows

Trade shows are a tried-and-true marketing tactic for increasing sales and building industry relationships. Companies can spend thousands of dollars and manhours attending shows, but a big investment doesn't necessarily guarantee a return. You need a guided strategy to engage visitors, capture leads and push them further through your marketing funnel.

1. **Invest time designing your display to be eye-catching and to work for you, not against you.** Trade show booths give you a minimum amount of space to make the biggest impression. It's almost like designing a tiny home where every piece needs to have a function or purpose. You may even opt to hire an interior designer rather than a booth design company to create a welcoming environment that integrates lead generation features such as scannable QR codes, space for swag takeaways and any fun or quirky pop-up activities you will use to grab attention.

2. **Tangible leads are the goal, but connection is more important.** Most sales aren't made on the showroom floor. While you are there, focus less on making a sale and more on forming sincere connections with visitors to your booth. In addition to your primary contact gathering method – whether that's via a contest giveaway, contact form, photo booth or any other number of lead capture tactics – keep a separate list of great connections and send them a personal follow-up after the show. Adding contacts to your company email list is good, but trade show visitors will have been added to a dozen email lists after the show and will likely spend the next week unsubscribing. Make sure they don't unsubscribe from you by giving them a personalized follow-up email or phone call to further the relationship.

3. **Take advantage of attending media.** Industry media flock to trade shows to keep tabs on the latest and greatest in their field. Show organizers should have a list of registered media

and are typically open to sharing it with PR pros or a brand representative. Take advantage of the opportunity by arranging media interviews during the show before you arrive. Even if they don't want to feature you in an immediate story, meet-and-greets are how positive media relationships are formed. They may have a busy schedule, so invite them to drop by your booth for a chat or a drink if they can't commit to a set meeting time.

4. **Don't forget about social.** While you're working the show floor, it can be easy to get wrapped up in conversations and forget to grab content for social media. Engaging with the show's social pages increases your chances of them re-posting your content from the show, furthering your reach to show attendees. Grab photos, video and use relevant hashtags to get the most out of the trade show experience.

5. **Online/In-Person hybrid events are the new norm.** For all its challenges, meeting online does have its perks. When an in-person show is sold out, ticket sales for the online livestream can still be running. If someone wants to attend a show but needs to be home for childcare, they can tune in from their couch. But people also still enjoy meeting in person when it's possible. Hybrid events will be the norm from now on and modern trade show marketing plans should take that into account.

TAKE ACTION: Create a trade show calendar with details about each event, including price to exhibit, expected attendance, marketing objective and a creative idea for enticing visitors into your booth.

See Also:
Challenge 14: Securing Interviews & Interview Prep
Challenge 27: Event Planning (Do's and Don'ts)
Challenge 30: Event Activations

Part IV: Stakeholder Communication

When we think about key stakeholders, groups like investors, consumers, board members, public officials and more may come to mind. One group that is often overlooked, however, are the employees just down the hall. This powerful group has the potential to either enhance or undermine your business.

Section 1: Internal Communications

If marketing is the practice of sharing a brand's story with consumers, "internal marketing" might seem counterintuitive. Why spend valuable time and resources marketing your company to a group of people who have already bought in? Internal communications has a broader goal if keeping all of your internal audiences engaged, energized and aligned with the brand's overall core values, whether it's your on-the-ground street team or the company's Board of Directors. Your internal stakeholders are just as important as your target customers.

Challenge 43: Developing an Employee Relations Plan

While you won't be sending targeted Facebook ads to your employees, an effective employee relations plan aims to promote a company's objectives, services, and greater mission to its team members – ultimately building loyalty and helping employees understand the "why" behind their work.

1. **Keep core values front and center.** Your core values serve as a mutual commitment by every member of the organization to act in a way that is consistent with your mission. As such, they should be woven throughout the fabric of any communications strategy. Perhaps you could regularly recognize team members who best exemplify your values, subsequently using this honor for shareable newsletter or social media content.

2. **Monitor internal sentiments.** Many companies have intranets, online groups, or private social media channels that are designated only for employees. These internal communications tools should be monitored regularly. Dialogue found on employee advocacy platforms can be a strong indicator of how employees are speaking about and representing the brand externally. Careful review of these sites can often reveal cracks in the foundation that can be addressed through your employee communication strategy.

3. **It may be time for an internal marketing campaign.** The reasons behind launching an internal marketing or employee relations campaign can vary from business to business. For some, positive employee sentiment is

lacking. For others, employee behavior does not match the promises the company makes to its customer base, so the organization needs to realign. Internal marketing can be used as a preventative tactic to retain top talent or simply to boost morale and brand education across the board.

4. **Internal marketing initiatives should feel truthful and representative of your employees' real experiences in the workplace.** For example, if your messaging includes language about offering a great work-life balance, but in reality, employees feel their work seeps into their personal lives, you need to adjust your language or address the problem internally. If you don't know if the message you've crafted is accurate, do some internal research to find out how employees really feel. Surveys are a great place to start. Make sure your team knows they should answer honestly, even if their feedback is not entirely positive.

5. **Tie internal marketing to large, institutional changes taking place, like new hires in the C-suite or a logo rebrand.** This will help current employees digest the new information and understand its roots. Just like an external campaign, implement your strategy in phases. In fact, you can apply many principles of consumer advertising to your internal marketing campaign.[15] Messaging should be consistent across channels and from all parties. Proper use of your typical brand voice and visuals is essential.

6. **Internal marketing is ultimately about having a unified brand vision, which means it reaches well beyond the marketing department.** As the people with the deepest understanding of the brand's mission, vision and values,

your marketing team is a natural choice for spearheading an internal marketing campaign. But don't forget to include human resources and public relations to support the campaign. Both have access to internal and external audiences that can be helpful in efficiently disseminating information.

TAKE ACTION: Assess your current internal communications plan. Is it lacking or even nonexistent? Look at what current initiatives you're implementing externally and find ways to bring those in-house to get your team excited and aligned with the organization's goals. Download a sample plan at www.reedpublicrelations.com/millennialsguide.

See Also:
Challenge 2: Working in the Industry
Challenge 10: Developing Key Messages
Challenge 36: Finding a Cause That Aligns With Your Brand
Challenge 46: Finding What Works Best for Your Team

Challenge 44: Establishing Effective Internal Communication Channels

The way you communicate with your employees should be authentic, honest and transparent, especially if the news is not all positive (i.e., budget cuts in order to implement a new green strategy). With thousands of team collaboration tools available online, it's crucial to understand how your team interacts on a day-to-day basis and what methods of communication they need to do their jobs efficiently.

1. **Distribute team communications through multiple channels.** Don't tether everyone to a text chain or email. Provide at least two ways for employees to always get in touch with each other. When making internal announcements, send a memo via email, then link to it in your internal messaging system. Or share news in person during your weekly team meeting and reiterate it via email. Utilize flyers, create a booklet and/or make a post in the employee Facebook group. Do your best to meet your team members where they are and provide multiple methods of communication.

2. **If you lead a team, set clear expectations for how your employees should communicate with you and others.** Should employees be reporting to their team leads once a day? Once a week? Be thorough in your job descriptions to set expectations on who should be communicated with whom and how often. Consider holding some form of regular in-person (or video) meeting to keep everyone connected face-to-face. This will help team members read each other's body language, hear sarcasm, or pick up on other tones that can be missed in written communications.

3. **Consider a two-way mentorship program in which older and younger employees can learn from each other.**[16] Younger team members can help teach technological literacy, while older employees can share their tips for in-person networking. This encourages relationships that might not otherwise be formed and will help all team members see the value that their counterparts bring to the table.

4. **Consistency is important for effective internal communications.** Too often, employees hear whisperings of new policies from co-workers then receive a completely different message from leadership a few weeks later. Your communicators should be a united front and share the same message across all channels and departments to maintain employee trust. Holding the occasional full-team marketing meeting that includes representatives from HR, PR, advertising, and sales can also help with consistency.

TAKE ACTION: Review the company's job descriptions for each role. Are reporting schedules and channels clearly defined?

See Also:
Challenge 9: Communications Audit
Challenge 56: Implementing Tools to Measure Your Success
Challenge 57: Actively Evaluating Your Progress

Challenge 45: Understanding Your Workplace Culture

What does workplace culture have to do with marketing? As Millennials and Generation Z take more and more of the market share, they're demanding companies live by the values they project to the rest of the world. It isn't enough to have splashy PR and marketing campaigns; today's consumers want to know the people behind the brand live and breathe what they are selling. Additionally, with top marketing talent in high demand, being able to effectively synopsize your culture and vision can be a valuable recruiting tool. To do this, you need to understand your workplace culture and how it ties into your overall marketing goals.

1. **What is workplace culture?** It refers to the set of shared values, attitudes and beliefs that your brand holds as a company. Workplace culture drives how employees and executives interact both internally with each other and externally with partners and consumers.

2. The Organizational Culture Assessment Instrument© (OCAI) is a research method used to assess organizational culture and explains four core types of workplace cultures:[17]
   - **Create Culture (Adhocracy)** centers on innovation and taking calculated risks by both employees and leaders alike. Experimenting is encouraged as companies with create culture often "fail forward" to come up with the next best thing.
   - **Collaborate Culture (Clan Culture)** aims to build a friendly work environment where leaders serve as mentors for younger staff to contribute to their personal and professional development. Teamwork and participation

are expected and success is measured by the level of care given to each client or customer.

- **Control Culture (Hierarchy Culture)** takes a more cautious approach with structured processes guiding the team's every action. The goal with control culture is to achieve stability by paying attention to details, being consistent and striving for efficiency in procedures.
- **Compete Culture (Market Culture)** focuses on getting results, getting them quickly and being better than the competition. This is typically a fast-paced work environment that emphasizing setting and meeting goals. PR and marketing firms often fall into compete culture.

3. **Keep core values front and center.** Your core values serve as a mutual commitment by every member of your organization to act in a way that is consistent with your mission. As such, they should be woven throughout the fabric of any communications strategy. Perhaps you could regularly recognize team members who best exemplify your values, subsequently using this honor for shareable newsletter or social media content.

4. **Show gratitude.** Regardless of the personality behind your organization, all workplace cultures thrive when you show gratitude. In a study from Harvard University and Wharton, receiving a "thank you" from a company boosted productivity by more than 50 percent.[18] Consider ways you can implement this into your communications plan, such as sharing appreciation and big wins every week at an all-team meeting or in your internal email newsletter. This is also an ideal time to reinforce your company mission and expectations by tying your gratitude back to a core value.

5. **Providing an excellent workplace and culture is key, but the work doesn't stop there.** Company leaders need to communicate to their workforce openly and frequently. This step is often skipped as decision-makers either assume everyone thinks the same way they do, or they are moving too quickly to share the details of a new service offering or change in company policy.

TAKE ACTION: With top executives at your company, determine which company culture fits your organization using the Organizational Culture Assessment Instrument. Then, in an all-team meeting, ask your employees, "What do we value here?" If their answer doesn't align with the workplace culture top execs identified, there may be a disconnect to address.

See Also:
Challenge 2: Working in the industry
Challenge 10: Developing key messages
Challenge 37: Implementing cause marketing campaigns
Challenge 43: Developing an employee relations plan

Challenge 46: Finding What Works Best for Your Team

For the first time in history, as many as five generations are working alongside one another.[19] Some people have grown up staring at screens, while others have spent the majority of their lives without cell phones. It comes as no surprise, then, that communication barriers abound between generations. To identify the best ways to communicate with your team – and the best ways for the team to communicate with each other – consider how generational differences affect how employees receive and process information.

1. **Compare spoken communication vs. written communication.** Before email—and fast Wi-Fi—was available at the office, employees relied on in-person interactions and phone calls to contact clients, customers, and their own team members. Baby Boomers, Generation X and Millennials all tend to prefer this type of communication. But individuals that grew up with the Internet, like Millennials and Generation Z, typically prefer to do business via email, text messages or direct messages. This divide can lead to some differences in the way communications are interpreted. A prime example is the use of ellipses in written communications. Boomers and Gen X were taught that an ellipsis can be used as a playful piece of punctuation to evoke mystery, while studies show Millennials and Gen Z interpret an ellipsis as a passive-aggressive statement.[19] Understanding the minutia behind generational speak can help you choose the best communication channels for your team to avoid unnecessary conflicts.

2. **You say tom-ay-to, I say tom-ah-to. They share a tomato emoji.** As time goes on, language changes and words or phrases can be interpreted in different tones. This phenomenon has been exacerbated by the addition of graphics to written communications. For example, a crying emoji can be used to

indicate something is sad, funny, or cute, depending on the context and its intended audience. Emojis, GIFs, and memes are all relatively new forms of communication that will resonate with some audiences but fall flat with others.

3. **Different generations have different expectations for response times.** Often, Boomers will send a note without the expectation of a same-day response. On the other hand, Gen Z is looking for lightning-fast responses to all types of communications. This can likely be attributed to how different generations communicated growing up. Some called their friends and waited hours or days for a response, while others have had texting capabilities at their fingertips since childhood. Setting clear expectations for response times will help your team avoid unnecessary tension.

4. **Get into the habit of just asking people their communication preferences.** Generalizations will only get you so far, so get to know each of your team members and personalize the way you get in touch with everyone.

TAKE ACTION: Issue a company survey to get a sense of what communication channels are working best for your team and where there might be communication gaps. Ask their thoughts on team collaboration tools such as Slack and Dropbox as well as general communications like emails and all-teams meetings.

See also:
Challenge 2: Working in the Industry
Challenge 44: Establishing Effective Internal Communication Channels
Challenge 48: Valuing Transparency
Challenge 56: Implementing Tools to Measure Your Success

Section 2: Crisis Communications

Product recalls, leadership scandals or even a global pandemic are just a few of the crises that may plague a company at one time or another. When an issue arises, your entire marketing strategy doesn't need to come to a halt, but there will likely be a need to pause, pivot and restart with modified messaging. A crisis can actually help a brand build credibility with customers when they see that the organization is addressing an issue directly and with transparency.

Challenge 47: Proactive Risk Management

No one expects to get a call that puts their organization's future in jeopardy—but things go wrong, incorrect information can go viral and the reputation of your brand can be at risk in a matter of minutes. In these situations, failing to plan is planning to fail. Especially for businesses that face intense scrutiny, things can escalate quickly.

1. **An astounding number of businesses don't have a crisis communications plan.** The steps to a crisis communications plan are not difficult, but they do require advance planning. Think of it as an insurance policy. You hope you'll never use it, but you'll sleep better knowing it's there. When it comes to crisis communications, there's no such thing as being too prepared.

2. **Establish the crisis management team.** In addition to the CEO, this should include key people from your PR team, legal counsel, and human resources. Determine a spokesperson and a back-up, and make sure they're media trained. A person's first experience in front of a live TV camera should not be in a time of crisis.

3. **Talk about what types of situations would threaten your organization.** What are your risk factors? This will vary by organization and there will likely be several. Discuss how you would respond. Write it down and develop messaging while you are thinking clearly. This will give you a much appreciated head start during a crisis.

4. **Identify your stakeholders – and the best way to get in front of them.** This could include employees, your board, customers, suppliers, media outlets and local government

officials. It's not enough to just know who they are. How will you reach them? Who warrants a personal phone call – and from which member of the crisis team? Is e-mail the best way to reach your customers?

5. **Reflect, refine, and reiterate.** Update your crisis communications plan regularly and evaluate its effectiveness after a crisis. Remember, a plan will only work if it is current. Task someone on your team with reviewing this at least quarterly and address any necessary changes, such as replacing a member of the crisis management team that has left the company or updating talking points for potential crisis scenarios. Post-crisis, look at what worked well and what processes or templates need to be updated to better handle the next crisis.

TAKE ACTION: Create a crisis communications plan or review your existing plan. Define the scenarios you will handle as a crisis and which situations you will handle as normal. What scope of reach/impact should an event have to call it a crisis? How severe does a situation need to be to consider it a crisis?

See Also:
Challenge 9 : Communications Audit
Challenge 15: Working With Media (Do's and Don'ts)
Challenge 29: Pivot! How to Adjust When Things Go Wrong
Challenge 44: Establishing Effective Internal Communication Channels

Challenge 48: Valuing Transparency

A guaranteed way to make a bad situation worse is by trying to cover it up. Millennials and Gen Z are tech-savvy and more skeptical of brands and government entities than previous generations. They're willing to do the research to hold brands accountable, and if you are hiding something, online sleuths will find it and share their discoveries on social media. Any crisis should be handled with honesty and integrity to ease the minds of the general public, your consumers and your team.

1. **Honesty leads to empathy.** Mistakes, natural disasters, and miscommunications happen. That's part of life and part of running a business. Your best defense is preparation and a quick response that explains what went wrong and the steps your organization is taking to fix it. Being open and honest with your audiences is key to winning over their forgiveness or support. Ultimately, crises that are handled swiftly and professionally by all members of the team can build customer loyalty and trust. Your customers will be able to sense the authenticity of your response.

2. **Build transparency into your crisis management plan.** A crisis communications plan that outlines the way you respond will result in better, more sincere statements. Guidelines for brand voice will help you develop statements that are written in a professional manner and not driven by emotion. Make it clear that transparency is a top priority regardless of the crisis at-hand.

3. **Transparency comes from the top down.** If your employees feel that they can't be honest when they make a genuine mistake, they are more likely to hide an issue that can fester into a full-blown disaster. Encourage your

team to be candid when things aren't going to plan so you can course-correct early or put measures in place to start reversing the damage. That means leadership must be willing to admit when they've made a mistake too and lead by example with clear communication and proactive steps to make it right.

TAKE ACTION: Determine the tool(s) you will use to monitor for brand crises and who is responsible for managing it. This can be as simple as setting up a Google news alert when your company's name is used in an online story or utilizing more in-depth brand management software that scans Internet chatter to gauge customer sentiment.

See Also:
Challenge 29: Pivot! How to Adjust When Things Go Wrong
Challenge 44: Establishing Effective Internal Communication Channels
Challenge 54: Practicing Ethical Marketing

Challenge 49: Focusing on Your Values and Priorities

Preserving brand integrity is a significant part of crisis management. Crises don't last forever, and it's important to think about how you want to be viewed after a crisis has passed. How you respond can affect your brand for years to come – well after a crisis has subsided.

1. **Think beyond the current stressful situation and act in a way that boosts your brand reputation, not diminishes it.** If a natural disaster strikes, do you want to be seen as a helpful resource or a passive bystander? If there's a scandal within your company, will you position your brand as honest and forthcoming or shady and conspiring? If you aren't sure where to start, always refer to the company's core values to guide your next steps.

2. **Define crisis for your organization.** Your crisis team doesn't need to be called in every time there's an angry tweet. Typically, a crisis can be defined by an event that disrupts standard business operations, threatens to harm your stakeholders, damages your reputation and/or negatively impacts your finances. Determine what constitutes an actual crisis for your organization and what should just be deferred to your customer service team.

3. **Have a crisis management plan ready to go.** A clear crisis plan can lead to faster response times, allowing your team to more quickly and easily "make the situation right" by offering the appropriate discount or other form of reparation that makes sense for your business. A faster crisis response time means fewer upset customers and allows you to better control the narrative without making rash decisions.

4. **Identify priority audiences.** Determine who needs to know what and when. In general, you will want to inform employees and internal stakeholders first so they can begin preparing to help your clients and customers when the news goes public. You also want to avoid your internal team resorting to speculation and rumors by being silent for too long. Externally, demonstrate concern for those affected and communicate what steps are being taken to solve the problem. Have someone on-call around the clock during the most intense hours or days following a crisis to make quick decisions and respond to media inquiries.

5. **Align your messaging and support your team.** It is crucial for everyone to know what message they should be always conveying. In your crisis plan, reinforce your brand's overall core messaging and distribute any situation-specific messaging in real time to avoid contradictions or confusion. Let your team know you have their backs and provide them with the tools they need to properly handle the situation.

TAKE ACTION: Define your brand's core messaging in your crisis communications plan. What are your brand's top values? What is your #1 value proposition to customers? How will you convey these messages during a crisis?

See Also:
Challenge 4: Your Message Matters – How Do You Know You're On the Right Track?
Challenge 43: Developing an Employee Relations Plan
Challenge 45: Understanding Your Workplace Culture
Challenge 54: Practicing Ethical Marketing

Challenge 50: Taking Control of the Story

In the best-case scenario, you'll never have to use your crisis management plan. But if you do, you want to get ahead of any misinformation and assumptions by responding swiftly, taking responsibility, and showing that your organization is taking actionable steps toward a solution.

1. **Your message and disposition matter.** How we act and appear to the world now has the potential to impact your brand for years to come — good or bad. Especially during a crisis, your message matters, both from you as a leader and your brand voice. Leaders set the standard for how others under their leadership behave. As we have all seen, fear is contagious, and your ability to keep calm and stay level-headed is critical.

2. **Have a crisis management plan in place.** "No comment" is the worst comment, but a prepared statement is far better than a thrown-together paragraph. Crisis planning gives you time to craft statements for the most likely scenarios and share them with team members for review. Even if you need to adjust the details in the moment, a prepared set of statements and a rough plan for how to distribute them will allow you to eloquently share your side of the story at a moment's notice.

3. **A crisis is not the time for off-the-cuff remarks or emails.** In times of crisis, saying the wrong thing can wreak havoc for your brand. Be thoughtful and deliberate. Refer to your crisis management plan and don't allow stress or emotions to stray you from your message. In this age of social media, anything you say or write could end up on the web.

4. **Don't be afraid to correct the record and set facts straight at any sign of misinformation.** Information travels quickly – even if it's

wrong. Work with your PR team to monitor media coverage and send corrections to reporters as needed. Keep tabs on the social conversation by monitoring your social media channels and promptly responding to direct messages and comments with questions. Avoid responding to individual comments on a media outlet's page (this can seem petty and defensive) but consider issuing a clarifying statement if you notice dozens of people coming to the wrong conclusion.

5. **Your team is your front line for crises.** They will likely be the people interacting directly with angry customers or fielding upset calls or emails. When negative feedback comes through—especially if it's from more than one customer—staff need to know what to do. Defining the escalation process and making it as easy as possible for team members will aid them in making quick decisions and avoiding communication delays. Plus, a clear crisis plan will empower your staff to be advocates for your business. They'll know you trust them to handle a crisis as outlined, which will set them up for success down the line.

TAKE ACTION: Assign specific roles within your crisis management plan to team members. These roles may include designating one person to speak to external audiences and another to keep internal stakeholders fully informed as well as who will take ownership for the overall strategy, who will oversee staffing social media conversations, etc.

See also:
Challenge 10: Developing Key Messages
Challenge 14: Securing Interviews and Interview Prep
Challenge 34: Securing Op-Eds and Speaking Opportunities
Challenge 47: Proactive Risk Management

Section 3: Community Relations

Community relations is an important facet of any business plan because organizations cannot operate without the support of the communities they serve. Community relations campaigns aim to connect with local entities such as schools, nonprofits, business associations, local officials and other community groups to both gain and give support in a way that is mutually beneficial.

Challenge 51: Launching Successful Grassroots Campaigns

Marketing pros love big, splashy ideas that get their brand in front of as many people as possible. There's certainly a time and a place for blanket brand awareness tactics, but some of the most meaningful consumer connections are formed when you go hyperlocal. Grassroots campaigns focus on highly targeted, engaging events that build relationships with a niche audience.

1. **Find your core audiences where they live, work and play.** Think about your ideal customer. Is your product or service specifically for men or women? Which age group and income bracket benefits from it? You might donate to silent auctions for the area's private schools if you want to get in front of affluent parents or host a complimentary happy hour for young professionals to appeal to local business leaders. Engaging the right audiences in practical ways will help ingrain your organization in the local community.

2. **Position your brand as a community partner and resource.** Community relations is possibly the least sales-y approach to marketing your business. It's less about making a sale and more about charming the public and being helpful to them. Become an ally for your consumers rather than just a faceless brand by demonstrating your investment in the local community.

3. **Make your call-to-action something people want to share.** Remember the ALS Ice Bucket Challenge? The viral trend had everyone from your next-door neighbor to international celebrities pouring water over their heads and sharing the videos on social media calling for others

to do the same – all in the name of raising awareness for Lou Gehrig's Disease. A key component to a grassroots campaign is getting your audience to share your messaging for you. Get creative with ways that consumers can complete a call-to-action while sharing your message with other people in their community.

TAKE ACTION: Identify 2 or 3 audiences you want to target with a grassroots campaign. Start a campaign plan by listing the objectives for engaging with each audience and how you will inspire them to naturally share your message throughout the campaign.

See also:
Challenge 8: Determining Target Audiences
Challenge 21: Finding Micro-Influencers to Fit Your Niche
Challenge 27: Event Planning (Do's and Don'ts)
Challenge 32: Implementing Cause Marketing Campaigns

Challenge 52: Public / Government Affairs

Policymakers use public affairs to gain support for their initiatives, improve their public image and inform their constituents about progress being made during their term. Companies and brands engage in public affairs to communicate requests for new or improved policies relevant to their industry, advocate for a cause important to their consumers or to publicly gain the support from someone in office. Knowing the ins and outs of government affairs is a specialization, but there are some key takeaways every millennial marketer should know.

1. **Do your research.** Government affairs is very much a data and research-based practice, and it's essential to track legislation related to your key issues on the city, state, and federal levels. Many states offer online bill tracking that will help your team keep an eye on amendments, committee meeting dates/reschedules, and new bills being introduced.

2. **You may need to register as a lobbyist.** If you are engaging with public officials as part of your marketing campaign, there's a good chance you are legally required to register as a lobbyist. The Federal Lobbying Act (1913) requires anyone aiding in the passage or defeat of legislation to register and report the amount of money he or she receives for lobbying activities.[20] Although lobbying laws vary by state, there could be legal repercussions for working with state lawmakers on legislation pieces without registering.

3. **Be careful with political contributions.** Familiarize yourself with statutes that dictate how you can give to a political campaign or figure as a business vs. as a public citizen. The Federal Corrupt Practices Act of 1925, Hatch Act of 1939 and the Taft-Hartley Act of 1947 prevent organizations from

contributing to any political campaign or candidate and prohibit any candidate from accepting such contributions.[20]

4. **Educate lawmakers as well as the public.** If a public policy issue affects your business operations, a key piece is education. Build relationships with your local officials and make sure they have a well-rounded understanding of your organization and the reason behind the policy change you are advocating for. In addition, educate the public about how it affects them and why they should support the policy. Encouraging your audiences to call, email or talk with their local lawmakers can be one of the most effective ways to get legislation changes made.

TAKE ACTION: Research your state lawmakers and put together a list of their stances on policies relevant to your organization.

See Also:
Challenge 12: Creating an Effective Media List
Challenge 34: Securing Op-Eds and Speaking Opportunities
Challenge 54: Practicing Ethical Marketing

Section 4: Cross-Cultural Communication

The world is a big place, but the Internet has made it feel a little smaller. Making the leap across cultures is a big step for a brand as traditions, dialects and values vary from place to place. Executing a marketing campaign that understands cultural differences takes time and research to do well.

Challenge 53: Preparing for International Campaigns

While global marketing campaigns have historically been reserved for massive moguls like Apple and Coca-Cola, the Internet allows even the smallest organization to share their message across continents. Going global is no easy feat, though, and marketing teams need to be strategic if they want to make waves across the pond.

1. **Determine target regions.** One of the first steps in developing an international marketing plan is to determine where your ideal customers are, both physically and digitally. Refer to your organization's growth plan to determine where you want to be recruiting new clients or customers then research how consumers in that country consume media and social media. You'll need to meet them where they are to capture their attention. For example, Chinese citizens primarily use WeChat to communicate while Americans still prefer Facebook or WhatsApp.[21] Identify where you want to be, and which communication tool is the local favorite.

2. **Get eyes and ears on the ground (when you can).** Understanding how consumers make purchasing decisions is at the core of any marketing campaign, but the decision-making process often changes from culture to culture. As often as possible, work with local agencies or consultants to ensure you are aligned with the local scene in your messaging and approach. It also helps to have people who can execute on the ground if you are doing anything outside of digital marketing on a global scale.

3. **Prepare for more competition.** One of the biggest challenges when expanding from a local marketing strategy to an

international one is the sheer competition. Not only will your actual product or service need to be superior, but you'll also have to get creative and have a great brand story to tell to break through the noise and get noticed. Research the competitors in each market, identify your differentiators and work those into your localized messaging for each region.

4. **Business operations should be ready to manage the extra exposure.** Sometimes more difficult than a marketing campaign that falls flat is one that is super successful – if you're not ready. Your organization needs to be equipped to handle the influx of traffic before making a global campaign push. This might include ordering extra supplies and materials, reviewing and improving processes for large-scale orders or inquiries, bringing on additional customer service team members, readying the website for increased traffic, and so much more.

TAKE ACTION: Before assembling your global growth strategy, work with your leadership team to determine why you want to expand to international marketing. Knowing the why will help you determine if going global is the right choice and assess your target markets if it is. Set 2 to 3 campaign goals that are aligned with the overall business goals of your organization in your outreach plan.

See Also:
Challenge 6: Be S.M.A.R.T! Setting Measurable Goals and Objectives
Challenge 8: Determining Your Target Audiences
Challenge 55: Pursuing Measurable Results

Section 5: Communication Ethics

Practicing ethical marketing is not only a moral issue but a legal one. Failing to uphold good communications ethics can damage a brand's reputation, lose customer trust and bring on lawsuits for false advertising, malpractice or even endangering public safety. Communication ethics should encompass all communication channels – both internal and external – to ensure your organization is communicating with integrity to its employees and its customers.

Challenge 54: Practicing Ethical Marketing

Public relations can have an unsavory reputation for "spin" – lying by omission or twisting the truth to position a brand in a way that isn't quite true – while marketers can get a bad rap for appropriating user data or promoting unverified claims. Fortunately, both industries have a clear code of ethics that should guide all marketing outreach.

1. **Honesty is top priority.** Both the American Marketing Association and Public Relations Society of America lead their codes of ethics with the call to be forthright and accurate in all communications with the public. Everything you share about the products, services, brands, or people you represent must be true and verifiable.

2. **Understand the ethics of journalism.** Often times, PR pros and marketers alike are working with journalists to share a brand's story. You want journalists to act with integrity, and that means avoiding conflicts of interest, refusing gifts for coverage, and seeking the whole truth without bias. Review the Society of Professional Journalists' Code of Ethics to get familiar with the ethics a journalist is bound to.[22]

3. **Take responsibility for the results of your marketing efforts.** While societal and cultural change can be considered monumental successes for your marketing campaigns, brands must accept the consequences of the marketing decisions and strategies they implement. This includes considering the social obligations a company might develop because of increased marketing and economic power. For example, if an organization grows to employ hundreds of thousands of people, it should pay those employees a livable wage.

4. **Maintain transparency.** Marketers must be diligent in promoting transparency within their organizations and to their external audiences. This includes everything from ensuring a brand influencer discloses that they were paid for an endorsement in their social media posts to reporting political campaign donations.

TAKE ACTION: Research a situation where a company has been in an ethically compromising situation and roleplay how your company would handle it. Review your internal code of ethics and implement training to ensure team members at all levels are operating with integrity and serving as a spokesperson for the company's core values.

See Also:
Challenge 2: Working in the Industry
Challenge 48: Valuing Transparency
Challenge 49: Focusing on Your Values and Priorities
Challenge 52: Public / Government Affairs

Part V: Evaluation

No marketing or PR campaign is complete without an evaluation stage. Evaluations should assess the effectiveness of the tactics used, compare expected results to the actual outcome and adjust for the next wave of outreach.

Challenge 55: Pursuing Measurable Results

Marketing is more traditionally linked to sales and consistently emphasizes data and measurement whereas PR strives to change the way people feel and think to build brand loyalty. Sentiment can be difficult to measure, and "how people feel" doesn't always get approved in budget meetings.

1. **Marketing success looks different for every organization.** Whether you are using an outside marketing agency or trying to align your internal marketing team, company leadership should be able to clearly communicate the brand's organizational goals and what they consider success. Use the overarching business goals to set S.M.A.R.T marketing goals with quantifiable KPIs.

2. **The value of PR and marketing can be defined by what is most important or useful to a brand's bottom line at a moment in time.** This means the metrics used to evaluate PR and marketing efforts often vary by company based on what the brand – and the leadership team – value most. For some executives, value comes in the form of seeing their name in the newspaper once a month. For others, it may be getting a certain number of new client calls each quarter. Therefore it is crucial to understand a brand's business goals and to set valuation metrics that align with those goals before launching a campaign.

3. **Measurable results lead to bigger budgets.** Executing a successful PR and marketing campaign is only half the battle. Afterward, you need to be able to communicate your success to the people making budgetary and business decisions. To do that, you will need to translate qualitative results into

quantitative – something measurable – to justify the investment and lock in funds for future marketing campaigns.

TAKE ACTION: Look at a past campaign plan and the postmortem report for that plan. Do you compare expected results with the outcome? Are your results in a narrative format or quantified showing an increased or decreased percentage in reach, followers, clicks, etc.? Then survey decision makers within your organization to find out which metrics are most important for them to see results for.

See also:
Challenge 6: Be S.M.A.R.T! Setting Measurable Goals and Objectives
Challenge 8: Determining Target Audiences
Challenge 12: Creating an Effective Media List
Challenge 23: Creating an Effective Landing Page

Challenge 56: Implementing Tools to Measure Your Success

If you are vying for a bigger piece of the budget against other departments at your organization, it's crucial to show the ROI in terms leadership execs understand. The right tools can help you do that by pulling data, tracking campaign benchmarks, and automating reports.

1. **Define your measurement of success at the start.** Perhaps you'd like to focus on hitting certain KPIs for engagement, or maybe you need to secure a certain amount of community partnerships. Whatever it may be, make sure you have specific, measurable goals in writing and are working toward them from day one. Additionally, make sure the KPIs you've selected to measure results support the ultimate organizational goals you've outlined. Irrelevant KPIs will only lead to off-track work, and that's not helping anyone.

2. **Link qualitative results to business goals to show value.** When you are aiming to change an audience's entire thought process, the shift can be difficult to show in hard numbers. One way to accomplish this is by tying each media placement, sponsorship, or other tactic directly to a business goal and end deliverable. This is particularly helpful when measuring success of PR campaigns and can provide support for what you *can* show hard numbers for such as readership and ad value equivalency.

3. **Choose the right software.** Hundreds of software options are available to help you track everything from audience demographics and social media engagement to website traffic and scrolling percentages. Choose tools that align with different areas of your marketing plan. Hootsuite™ is ideal for

scheduling and measuring social media posts while Semrush is great for web traffic analytics. You will have to invest in a pro plan for most in-depth measurement tools, but some of them are free or have free lite versions like Google Analytics and HubSpot.

TAKE ACTION: Assign someone on your team to set up trials with 2 to 3 new marketing measurement software tools. Test drive each tool and find one that best suits your needs before investing in a paid version.

See Also:
Challenge 6: Be S.M.A.R.T! Setting Measurable Goals and Objectives
Challenge 39: Knowing When to Pursue Paid Opportunities
Challenge 55: Pursuing Measurable Results

Challenge 57: Actively Evaluating Your Progress

Effective campaigns can take time to start showing results, and it's important to set those expectations with your team and executive leadership, but you should also be keeping tabs on progress as you go.

1. **Don't wait to adjust or salvage resources by redirecting.** Report progress regularly and be willing to change your approach if you aren't hitting the metrics you set out to. Setting goals and walking away is a surefire way to get budgets cut when a campaign is underperforming and you don't realize it until it's too late. Yes, stopping a campaign midway is a headache, but it's better than showing poor returns on your company's investment in a post-mortem report. Instead, develop procedures that measure progress along the way to earn optimal results and higher ROI.

2. **Measurement should be fluid as campaigns and business goals change.** The metrics that make sense this year may be different next year or even quarter to quarter. They should certainly change based on the initiatives you are rolling out. Measurable objectives could be several media hits, new client leads, email sign-ups or social media audience reach. Establish these metrics before a campaign begins so you know what marks you must hit and what value they hold.

3. **Be diligent about staying in-budget.** Sometimes PR, advertising and marketing get a bad rap for ignoring budgets and encouraging over-the-top activations that result in little more than buzz. While it's great to be creative and embrace a good stunt, your marketing/PR spend has to be justifiable and tracked along the way. Success comes when your creative ideas

and the costs to execute them successfully align. If, at the end of the day, your cost per customer acquisition or conversion is so high that you've lost money, all the buzz in the world won't make up for it. Establish a weekly budget review for new initiatives to ensure you aren't exceeding the limit within the first two weeks.

TAKE ACTION: Consider your current evaluation methods and build out a reporting schedule that measures success on a weekly or biweekly basis. Junior-level team members can pull data and highlight red flags, but a higher-level employee should have an active hand in reviewing results throughout execution.

See Also:
Challenge 6: Be S.M.A.R.T! Setting Measurable Goals and Objectives
Challenge 29: Pivot! How to Adjust When Things Go Wrong
Challenge 44: Establishing Effective Internal Communication Channels

Acknowledgements

The authors would like to thank Macey Cleary Binner, Shane Tinnin, and Evane Stoner for reviewing this book.

Public Relations Society of America (APR Study Guide)
American Marketing Association
Society of Professional Journalists
REED Public Relations Blog: www.reedpublicrelations.com

References

1. Scott M. Cutlip, Allen H. Center, Glen M. Broom, *Effective Public Relations,* 11th Edition (Pearson, 2013).
2. "APR Study Guide - Public Relations Society of America." Public Relations Society of America. https://www.prsa.org/docs/default-source/accreditation-site/apr-study-guide.pdf?sfvrsn=3023e23c_2.
3. "The Peso Model." Spin Sucks, September 27, 2021. https://spinsucks.com/the-peso-model/.
4. "Definitions of Marketing." American Marketing Association. https://www.ama.org/the-definition-of-marketing-what-is-marketing/.
5. Walker, Mason. "U.S. Newsroom Employment Has Fallen 26% since 2008." Pew Research Center. Pew Research Center, July 16, 2021. https://www.pewresearch.org/fact-tank/2021/07/13/u-s-newsroom-employment-has-fallen-26-since-2008/.
6. Auxier, Brooke, and Monica Anderson. "Social Media Use in 2021." Pew Research Center: Internet, Science & Tech. Pew Research Center, April 9, 2021. https://www.pewresearch.org/internet/2021/04/07/social-media-use-in-2021/.
7. "Video Marketing Statistics: New Data for 2022." Wyzowl, December 2021. https://www.wyzowl.com/video-marketing-statistics/.
8. "What Is Digital Marketing?" American Marketing Association, October 4, 2021. https://www.ama.org/pages/what-is-digital-marketing/.
9. "Metaverse Market size worth $824.53 Billion, Globally, by 2030 at 39.1% CAGR: Verified Market Research®." PR Newswire, July 13, 2022. https://www.prnewswire.com/news-releases/metaverse-market-size-worth--824-53-billion-globally-by-2030-at-

39-1-cagr-verified-market-research-301585725.html#:~:text=Metaverse%20Market%20size%20worth%20%24%20824.53,CAGR%3A%20Verified%20Market%20Research%C2%AE

10. "Gen Z Has $360 Billion to Spend, Trick Is Getting Them to Buy." Bloomberg U.S. Edition, November 2021. https://www.bloomberg.com/news/articles/2021-11-17/gen-z-has-360-billion-to-spend-trick-is-getting-them-to-buy?leadSource=uverify%20wall.
11. "7 Surprising Stats about the Underappreciated Power of Thought Leadership." LinkedIn, December 16, 2018. https://www.linkedin.com/business/marketing/blog/linkedin-ads/7-surprising-stats-about-the-underappreciated-power-of-thought.
12. "The Deloitte Global Millennial Survey: A Decade in Review." Deloitte, 2021. https://www2.deloitte.com/content/dam/Deloitte/global/Documents/2021-deloitte-global-millennial-survey-decade-review.pdf.
13. Girija Swaraj, Pasupuleti, and Sumit Kumar Chaudhuri. "Celebrity Endorsement: Through the Ages." IBS Case Development Center, 2004.
14. Winn, Ross. "2021 Podcast Stats & Facts (New Research from APR 2021)." Podcast Insights®, December 28, 2021. https://www.podcastinsights.com/podcast-statistics/.
15. Mitchell, Colin. "Selling the Brand Inside." Harvard Business Review, August 1, 2014. https://hbr.org/2002/01/selling-the-brand-inside.
16. Wong, Kellie. "5 Ways to Bridge the Generation Gap Between Employees ." Engage Blog, March 12, 2020. https://www.achievers.com/blog/5-ways-to-bridge-the-generation-gap-between-employees/.
17. Cameron, Kim, and Robert Quinn. "About the Organizational Culture Assessment Instrument (OCAI)." OCAI Online. Accessed January 27, 2022.

https://www.ocai-online.com/about-the-Organizational-Culture-Assessment-Instrument-OCAI.

18. "The Big Benefits of a Little Thanks." Harvard Business Review, March 30, 2015. https://hbr.org/2013/11/the-big-benefits-of-a-little-thanks.
19. Pelta, Rachel. "Breaking Barriers: Communication Between Generations in the Workplace." FlexJobs Blog. FlexJobs.com, September 3, 2020. https://www.flexjobs.com/blog/post/workplace-generational-communication-gaps/.
20. "APR Study Guide - Public Relations Society of America." Public Relations Society of America. https://www.prsa.org/docs/default-source/accreditation-site/apr-study-guide.pdf?sfvrsn=3023e23c_2.
21. "World Map of Social Networks." Vincos Blog, January 27, 2022. https://vincos.it/world-map-of-social-networks/.
22. "SPJ Code of Ethics - Society of Professional Journalists." Society of Professional Journalists, September 6, 2014. https://www.spj.org/ethicscode.asp.

About the Authors

Lauren Reed

There was no parachute. When Lauren quit her job as a senior director at a national PR and marketing agency, she jumped without a net. There was no next job lined up. No lucrative book deal signed. No beach villa in St. Tropez waiting for her new life as a trophy wife. Lauren didn't need any of that. She had faith in herself. Faith that she would stick the landing. No safety net or parachute needed. Within a few weeks – yes, weeks – she'd started REED Public Relations and had a roster of amazing clients. Just like that, the agency was well on its way to making a lasting impact on the Nashville PR scene.

Industry accolades back up Lauren as a rising star. She earned her Accreditation in Public Relations (APR) designation in 2010 and is a member of the Entrepreneurs' Organization, former president of PRSA Nashville and recipient of the PRSA Nashville 2011 Mercury Award, which recognizes the top young PR professional in the Nashville market. Most recently, Lauren was named to the *Nashville Business Journal*'s 40 Under 40, and its Most Admired CEO list in 2018, 2019, 2020, 2021, 2022, and 2023. REED PR has also been named one of the Business Journal's Best Places to Work multiple times.

Even with all of her awards and the tremendous work she has done, she still says one of her greatest professional accomplishments was creating REED PR's Be The Good program, which reserves a portion of the agency's revenue to provide travel grants to individuals who want to do volunteer or mission work at home or abroad.

Email: lauren@reedpublicrelations.com
Website: www.reedpublicrelations.com

Jennifer Poythress

Jennifer Poythress is a leader in metaverse marketing and virtual communications as founder and project lead at The Rabbit Hole Virtual Marketing.

Jennifer's expertise has a foundation in journalism. As a writer for *The Knoxville News Sentinel* and Reuters, she earned her stripes in AP Style and news writing one column inch at a time. Jennifer made the leap to public relations and marketing by joining Nashville-based agency REED Public Relations in 2014. During her time at REED, Jennifer led multifaceted, award-winning campaigns for clients in the food and beverage, senior living and professional services categories before becoming an internal marketing manager for the agency.

In 2017, Jennifer launched The Rabbit Hole VR as the Southeast's first virtual reality gaming center that has been featured in outlets like Inc.com and the *Nashville Business Journal.* The Rabbit Hole later launched a Virtual Marketing division, combining Jennifer's PR & marketing acumen with the hands-on experience of introducing everyday people to immersive tech at the arcade locations.

The Rabbit Hole Virtual Marketing now specializes in developing and executing unique marketing solutions for brands using VR, AR, and AI.

Email: jennifer@therabbitholevr.com
Website: https://www.rabbithole-marketing.com

Made in United States
Troutdale, OR
11/03/2026

56845376R00116